Collins

OCR GCSE Revision

Computer Science

Computer Science

OCR GCSE

Revision Guide

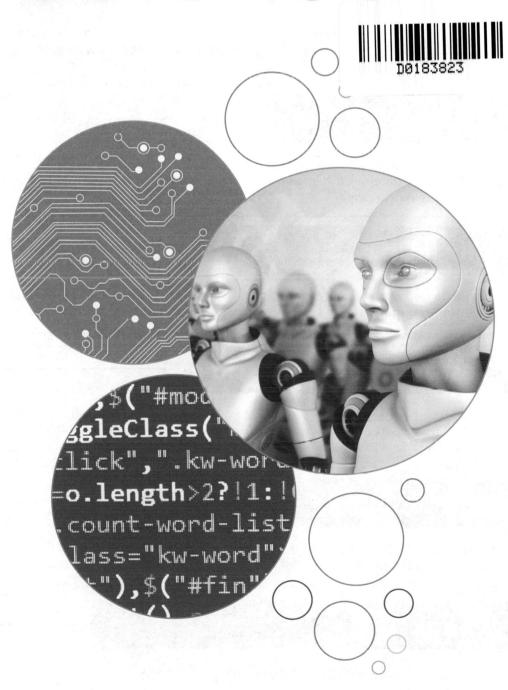

D0183823

Paul Clowrey

How to use this Book

Revise

These pages provide a recap of everything you need to know for each topic.

You should read through all the information before taking the Quick Test at the end. This will test whether you can recall the key facts.

Quick Test

1. Which act was specifically designed to prosecute hackers?
2. If a reporter would like to know how much a local council has spent on expenses, which act would apply?
3. Which act would prevent customer lists being sold to another business outside the EEA without permission?

Practise

These topic-based questions appear shortly after the revision pages for each topic and will test whether you have understood the topic. If you get any of the questions wrong, make sure you read the correct answer carefully.

Review

These topic-based questions appear later in the book, allowing you to revisit the topic and test how well you have remembered the information. If you get any of the questions wrong, make sure you read the correct answer carefully.

Mix it Up

These pages feature a mix of questions for the different topics. They will make sure you can recall the relevant information to answer a question without being told which topic it relates to.

Test Yourself on the Go

Visit our website at www.collins.co.uk/collinsGCSErevision and print off a set of flashcards. These pocket-sized cards feature questions and answers so that you can test yourself on all the key facts anytime and anywhere. You will also find lots more information about the advantages of spaced practice and how to plan for it.

Workbook

This section features even more topic-based questions as well as practice exam papers, providing two further practice opportunities for each topic to guarantee the best results.

ebook

To access the ebook revision guide visit

www.collins.co.uk/ebooks

and follow the step-by-step instructions.

Contents

Contents

Computational Thinking, Algorithms and Programming

The Purpose and Function of the Central Processing Unit

You must be able to:

- Describe the purpose of the CPU
- Describe common CPU components and their function
- Describe the main concepts of von Neumann architecture.

What is the Central Processing Unit For?

- The **central processing unit** (CPU), also known as a microprocessor, is the 'brain' at the core of any computer system.
- All computer systems have the following three basic elements:
  1. **Input** – information, or data, feeds into the system from **input devices** such as keyboards, mice, cameras or sensors.
  2. **Process** – the information collected needs to be processed and actions need to be carried out. This may mean carrying out calculations, sending instructions to other devices or transferring information from different areas of memory.
  3. **Output** – once processed or acted on, the result is presented via **output devices** such as monitors, speakers, mechanical movement or printers.
- The CPU is where this processing takes place, and modern processors are based on **von Neumann architecture** or structure.

Key Point

The CPU processes information and instructions, and coordinates the flow of data around a system.

Common Central Processing Unit Components

- Modern CPUs contain the following key elements:
  - The **arithmetic logic unit** (ALU) is where calculations are carried out. These include mathematical tasks, logic tests and data comparisons.
  - The **control unit** controls the flow of data around the system, both inside the CPU and between input and output devices. Control signals are sent to the ALU, cache and memory registers.
  - **Cache** is a small area of very fast memory within the CPU used to store data when carrying out instructions. Having access to this additional area prevents data bottlenecks when communicating with RAM and secondary storage (covered later in this chapter).

von Neumann Architecture

- The original design on which modern computers are based was created by mathematician **John von Neumann** in 1945.
- The diagram shown below is based on his design for a 'stored program' computer system. This means that both the computer program and the data it processes are stored in memory.

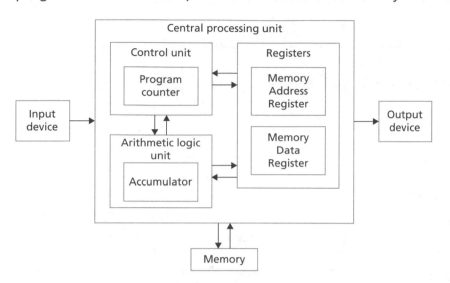

- Key aspects of von Neumann architecture include:

  - **Memory Address Register** (MAR) – this is the location address in memory of the next piece of data or instruction that the CPU needs to be fetched or stored.
  - **Memory Data Register** (MDR) – an instruction or piece of data fetched from memory is stored here temporarily until it is used.
  - **Program counter** – this continuously provides the CPU with the memory address of the next instruction in the cycle to be carried out.
  - **Accumulator** – this is where the results of calculations carried out by the ALU are temporarily stored until they are needed.
  - **Bus** – a physical pathway shared by signals to and from components of a computer system such as input and output devices. The arrows in the diagram represent wires and circuit boards.

Key Words

central processing unit
input devices
output devices
von Neumann architecture
arithmetic logic unit
control unit
cache
Memory Address Register
Memory Data Register
program counter
accumulator
bus

Quick Test

1. Which key element of the CPU carries out logic tests?
2. Define the term 'bus'.
3. Name four input devices.

Systems Architecture

You must be able to:

- Explain the process of fetching and executing instructions
- Explain how the characteristics of a CPU affect its performance
- Describe the purpose and examples of embedded systems.

The Fetch–Decode–Execute Cycle

- The fetch–decode–execute cycle, often referred to as just the fetch–execute cycle, describes how the CPU:
  1. fetches instructions
  2. decodes them
  3. carries out (or executes) the instructions.

Fetch: The processor fetches the instruction from memory and uses the program counter to keep track of where it is.

Execute: The instruction is then carried out; this could be a calculation or the transfer of data.

Decode: Once the instruction is loaded, the CPU needs to know what it means, so the instruction must be decoded.

Common Central Processing Unit Characteristics

- The performance of a CPU can be affected by several elements:
  - **clock speed**
  - cache size
  - number of **cores**.
- **Clock speed** refers to the rate at which instructions are processed by the CPU.
  - A 3-GHz (gigahertz) CPU can perform three billion cycles per second.

- **Cache size** – to prevent **data bottlenecks**, cache memory within the CPU allows temporarily stored data to be accessed very quickly.
  - Modern CPUs may have two or more levels of cache, and once these have been used the CPU will then use the computer's main memory, which is much slower.
  - The L1 cache is used to store very frequently accessed data – it is quite small but very fast.
  - The L2 cache is slower and further away but is still more efficient than the main memory.
- **Number of cores** – rather than continuously increase the speed of a single processor, modern CPUs now contain multiple processors on the same chip.
  - This is referred to as a multicore processor, and each core can carry out separate tasks simultaneously.
  - A dual core has two cores and a quad core has four cores.

> **Key Point**
>
> Multicore processors have more than one processor on the same CPU.

What are Embedded Systems?

- A small computer with a specific task within a larger device is an **embedded system**.
- Examples include:
  - the programme control of a dishwasher
  - the Internet connectivity system within a liquid crystal display (LCD) television.

> **Key Point**
>
> Embedded systems can be found within electronic devices that have multiple functions.

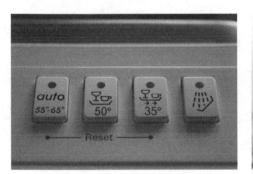

> **Quick Test**
>
> 1. What is the speed of a CPU measured in?
> 2. How does a multicore CPU help a computer to run faster?
> 3. Name three devices in a modern office that contain embedded systems and the tasks that those systems may carry out.

> **Key Words**
>
> clock speed
> cores
> data bottlenecks
> embedded system

Memory

You must be able to:

- Understand the difference between RAM and ROM
- Describe the purpose of RAM and ROM in a computer system
- Explain the need for virtual memory
- Describe what flash memory is.

What are Random Access Memory and Read-Only Memory?

- **RAM** (random access memory) is a temporary area that a computer uses to store data in current use.
  - It is much quicker to access than the computer's hard drive.
  - It acts like our short-term memory, quickly recalling important information.
  - The two types of RAM are DRAM (dynamic RAM) and SRAM (static RAM).
- **ROM** (read-only memory) provides a computer system with important instructions that do not change.
  - The instructions are permanently programmed into a chip and will have specific functions.

What is the Difference between Random Access Memory and Read-Only Memory?

- Both RAM and ROM are stored on chips within the computer system, but there are key differences between them:
  - RAM is **volatile**, meaning that once power is switched off all data stored on it is lost.
  - ROM **permanently** keeps the instructions written at manufacture.
  - Access to ROM is much slower than access to RAM.
  - RAM storage capacity is usually in the order of gigabytes.
  - ROM storage capacity is much smaller.

> **Key Point**
>
> RAM is volatile; ROM is permanent (or non-volatile).

Why Does a Computer System Need Random Access Memory and Read-Only Memory?

- When browsing the Internet, playing games or performing calculations, instructions and data need to be accessed quickly and RAM is much quicker to access than the hard drive.
- Information stored in RAM is placed in known storage locations by the CPU, and the CPU can access these locations in any order, speeding up the system.

- When a computer starts, or boots, the first set of instructions accessed is the **BIOS** (basic input/output system) and this is stored within ROM chips. The BIOS ensures that all essential hardware can communicate effectively and launch the operating system.
- Because ROM is permanent, designers place important instructions on it to ensure that these cannot be edited when the BIOS is used.

What is Virtual Memory?

- Running multiple applications on a modern computer system (e.g. working, browsing and playing music) will quickly fill the RAM.
- If the RAM becomes full the system will slow, so **virtual memory** is created to help.
- Part of the hard drive memory is designated as temporary RAM, or virtual memory, and non-essential data stored in RAM is transferred to the hard drive.
- As access to the hard drive memory is slower than access to RAM, the system will slow if it is relied on too heavily.

What is Flash Memory?

- **Flash memory** was developed from early ROM chips and is both programmable and **erasable**.
- Unlike with RAM, data stored on flash memory will remain when power is disconnected, making flash memory ideal for portable storage solutions.
- Flash memory is now commonplace within digital devices and as separate storage such as:
  - smartphone and digital camera storage
  - SD (secure digital) cards
  - SSD (solid-state drive) laptop hard drives, replacing traditional magnetic drives
  - USB connected portable hard drives.
- Some computers now use flash memory instead of ROM to store BIOS; this allows BIOS to be upgraded by the manufacturer to add system improvements.
- Although flash memory is more expensive, its durability, size and speed mean that it is replacing many optical and magnetic storage solutions.

Key Point

Flash memory has fast data access, is light and has no moving parts.

Key Words

RAM
ROM
volatile
BIOS
virtual memory
erasable

Quick Test

1. Does a computer system use RAM or ROM for the temporary storage of data?
2. Why will a system create virtual memory?
3. Name three features of flash memory that make it more desirable than magnetic storage.

Storage Types, Devices and Characteristics

You must be able to:

- Describe the need for secondary storage
- Explain the term 'data capacity'
- Describe common types of storage media and devices and their characteristics
- Explain the most suitable choice of storage device for a given application.

What is Secondary Storage and Why Do We Need It?

- Away from the CPU and motherboard, **secondary storage** refers to the devices used to store programs, documents and files.
- These devices need to be **non-volatile**, otherwise we would need to install programs every time we wanted to use them.
- Data is stored magnetically, optically or electronically (SSD using flash memory).

Key Point

Non-volatile secondary storage means that data is still intact when the power source is removed.

Data Capacity and File Size

- The choice of secondary storage depends on the capacity of the device compared with the file size of the data to be stored.
- Common **storage capacities** are described in the tables on the next page and are based on the following units of measurement:

– 1 character	=	1 bit
– 4 bits	=	1 nibble
– 8 bits	=	1 byte
– 1000 bytes	=	1 kilobyte (KB)
– 1000 kilobytes	=	1 megabyte (MB)
– 1000 megabytes	=	1 gigabyte (GB)
– 1000 gigabytes	=	1 terabyte (TB)
– 1000 terabytes	=	1 petabyte (PB)

- Please note that you may also see sizes referred to as 1024 rather than 1000. This is because 1024 is a power of 2 in relation to binary calculations.

Comparing Secondary Storage Media

- Optical, magnetic and SSD secondary storage devices can be categorized by their properties to help decide on the most appropriate storage device for any situation.
- Characteristics used to compare devices are capacity, speed, portability, durability, reliability and cost.

Key Point

Although visually very similar, optical discs come in many different formats.

Magnetic storage	Technology	Advantages
	Hard drives contain spinning magnetic discs, accessed by an arm that moves across the surface to read and write data.	• High capacity at a low cost. • Fast data access.
	Common usage • Desktop PCs. • **Network storage**. • Backup systems. • Large document files.	**Disadvantages** • The disk will eventually fail. • Easily damaged, resulting in corruption of data. • Large physical size. • Complex moving parts.

Optical storage	Technology	Advantages
	A track of pits spirals from the centre to the edge of the disc. Read by a laser and lens, this pattern is converted into binary data stream that can contain digital text, images, sound and video.	• Cheap to manufacture. • Very portable. • Widely available.
	Common usage • Storing music, video and games. • CD (compact disc) 700 MB. • DVD (digital versatile disc) 4.7–9.4 GB. • Blu-ray 25–128 GB.	**Disadvantages** • Discs can be damaged easily and degrade over time. • Limited capacity. • Compatibility issues between players.

SSD storage	Technology	Advantages
	A grid of electrical cells divided into sections called pages and then into **blocks** are used to send and receive data.	• Faster read/write access than magnetic storage. • Small size. • No moving parts. • Ideal for USB (Universal Serial Bus) and other portable devices.
	Common usage • USB portable drives. • Smartphone and digital camera memory. • Laptop hard drives.	**Disadvantages** • More expensive per GB than magnetic or optical storage. • Can wear out over time.

Quick Test

 1. Give three reasons why games consoles use optical discs to store games.
2. Why is a magnetic hard drive not very durable?
3. Name five portable uses of SSDs.

Key Words

secondary storage
non-volatile
storage capacities
network storage
blocks

Where space is not provided, write your answers on a separate piece of paper.

The Purpose and Function of the Central Processing Unit

1 Which part of the body is the CPU often compared to? [1]

2 For each device, place a tick in **one** of the columns to indicate whether the device feeds into the CPU or receives instructions from it. [6]

Device	Input	Output
Keyboard		
Printer		
Monitor		
Webcam		
Sensor		
Speakers		

3 In which CPU component are calculations carried out? [1]

4 What is the small area of very fast memory within the CPU known as? [1]

5 Describe the control unit. [1]

6 Define the term 'stored program'. [2]

7 Name the **two** registers within the von Neumann model. [2]

8 Complete the following sentence:

The area within the ALU that stores the results of calculations until needed is called the

_____. [1]

9 Which aspect of von Neumann architecture continuously provides the CPU with the memory address of the next instruction? [1]

10 In which decade was the von Neumann design created? [1]

Systems Architecture

1 Match each term with its description. [3]

Fetch	The instruction is decoded to enable it to be understood.
Decode	The instruction is carried out.
Execute	The instruction is brought from memory.

2 CPU clock speed is measured in _____. [1]

3 How many cores does a quad-core processor have? [1]

4 Complete the following sentence:

If a CPU becomes overwhelmed with instructions and calculations, a _____ can occur. [1]

5 Which is faster, the L1 cache or the L2 cache? [1]

6 A 2-GHz CPU will carry out how many cycles per second when processing instructions? [1]

7 What is the main benefit of multicore processors? [1]

8 List **three** devices that may contain an embedded system. [3]

9 Describe a potential use for an embedded system in:

a) a smart TV [1]

b) a washing machine. [1]

Memory

1 What do the abbreviations RAM and ROM stand for? [2]

2 Which of RAM and ROM is a temporary storage area? [1]

3 Which of RAM and ROM permanently holds specific functions? [1]

4 Define the term 'volatile memory'. [2]

5 Which of RAM and ROM is volatile? [1]

6 Access to ROM is slower than access to RAM. True or false? [1]

7 What does the abbreviation BIOS stand for? [1]

8 When is the BIOS normally accessed? Tick **one** box.

   A When a new program is installed. ☐

   B When the computer boots up. ☐

   C As the computer shuts down. ☐ [1]

9 When is virtual memory needed? [1]

10 Why is virtual memory slower than standard RAM? [1]

11 *Flash memory is volatile.* True or false? [1]

12 Name **two** devices that use flash memory. [2]

13 Describe **three** benefits of flash memory over magnetic storage. [3]

Storage Types, Devices and Characteristics

1 Why does secondary storage need to be non-volatile? [1]

2 List **three** methods of storing data. [3]

3 1000 megabytes is called a .... [1]

4 When using units of bytes it is commonly accepted that the '24' can be ignored and that data capacities are described to the nearest 1000. True or false? [1]

5 Put the following in order of size, from smallest to largest:

TB, KB, GB, MB [1]

6 List **six** characteristics used to compare secondary storage devices. [6]

7 Which type of optical storage has a standard range of capacities of 4.7–9.4 GB? [1]

8 Which storage type is the most expensive per GB? [1]

9 State **two** reasons why SSDs are ideal for portable USB devices. [2]

10 Describe **two** considerations to be made when storing important files for long periods of time. [2]

11 Name the most common type of storage in desktop computers. [1]

Common System Threats

You must be able to:

- Describe a variety of common threats to computer networks
- Describe the potential dangers of each threat method
- Explain how criminals exploit our trust to access information.

Why are Networks Attacked?

- Computer networks are now a part of our homes, schools, and places of work and leisure.
- Personal, business and financial information is extremely valuable and is traded between criminals around the world.
- Stolen usernames and passwords allow criminals to access bank accounts and private information, which means that they can potentially commit crimes against us without our knowledge.

> **Key Point**
>
> Personal information is traded across the world by criminals wanting to access our online accounts.

Malware

- **Malware** is short for 'malicious software', and describes a piece of software designed to breach security or damage a system.
- Types of malware include:

Virus	A program hidden within another program or file, designed to cause damage to file systems.
Worm	A malicious program that acts independently and can replicate itself and spread throughout a system.
Trojan	Installed by a user thinking it is a legitimate piece of software when, in fact, it will cause damage or provide access for criminals.
Spyware	Secretly passes information on to a criminal without the user's knowledge. It is often packaged with free software.
Adware	Displays targeted advertising and redirects search requests without permission.
Ransomware	Limits or denies a user access to their system until a ransom is paid to unlock it.
Pharming	The redirecting of a user's website – by modifying their Domain Name System (DNS) entries – to a fraudulent site without their permission.

Social Engineering

- Throughout history, con artists have tried to trick people into giving up personal information or valuables.
- These **social engineering** methods have developed into computer-based scams that prey on the good nature of users and pretend to be from a trusted organization or contact.

- **Phishing** uses email, text messages and phone calls to impersonate, for example, a financial organization and ask users to confirm or divulge personal details. These details can be used to access and steal from online accounts.
- **Shouldering** is the technique of watching a user at an ATM (automated teller machine) (cash machine) and recording their PIN (personal identification number) details.
- **Blagging** is carried out face to face and uses believable scenarios to trick people into giving up personal information.

Key Point

Scams are not just limited to desktop email, but can also be sent to our smartphones and tablets.

Threats Aimed Directly at Large Networks

- Large organizations and businesses are often the victims of attacks that try to access their computer systems to steal large quantities of data or inflict major damage.
  - A **brute force attack** repeatedly tries different usernames and passwords in an attempt to access a system.
  - A **denial of service (DoS) attack** tries to flood a website or network with data traffic to bring it to a halt. Such attacks are often used to demand a ransom or a change in policy.
  - **Data interception and theft** is the method of intercepting and decoding a message containing sensitive information before it reaches its destination.
  - **SQL injection** uses the same Structured Query Language used to manage large databases to attack them. Commands written in this language are used instead of usernames and passwords to access and steal private information.
- A poor network policy that does not set rules about how users may access and share information within a system can leave that system open to attack.

Key Words

malware
virus
worm
Trojan
spyware
adware
ransomware
pharming
social engineering
phishing
shouldering
blagging
brute force attack
denial of service (DoS) attack
data interception and theft
SQL injection

Quick Test

1. Name five types of malware.
2. What is shouldering?
3. What tips would you offer to someone using an ATM for the first time?
4. What does DoS attack stand for?

Threat Prevention

You must be able to:

- Describe how users and organizations can prevent threats
- Explain how networks can be tested to identify potential threats
- Describe how to increase computer system security.

How Can We Protect Ourselves?

- The protection of our computer systems has to constantly evolve to meet the ever-increasing number of threats.
- The threats are from various sources, such as computer users with criminal intent and automated self-replicating virus programs.

Computer-Based Protection and Detection

- **Firewalls:**
  - control the transmission of data between a computer and other network computers or the Internet
  - can be configured to apply rules to certain programs, websites or network connections
  - can be either software based or hardware based – a hardware firewall is generally more expensive but more robust.

- **Anti-malware:**
  - is designed to spot a malicious virus, worm, Trojan, adware or spyware program and to remove it from a system or network
  - must be regularly updated to meet the latest threats that appear on a daily basis.
- **Encryption:**
  - converts information using a **public encryption key** into a meaningless form that cannot be read if intercepted
  - the only way to decrypt the information is with a **private key** or **cypher** generated by the owner
  - the encrypted text and the cypher are never transmitted together.

Managed Protection and Testing

- **Network policies** are written by the owners of large networks to set practical rules that all users should follow. These can relate to password privacy, the use of personal devices, the backing up of data and acceptable network use.

- **Network forensics** monitors and records network traffic to make sure that any attacks can be analysed and that the resulting information can be used in subsequent investigations.
- **Penetration testing** is used to find potential problems and vulnerabilities within a system that could be exploited for criminal purposes.

Security Issues and Computer Users

- Users are usually the weakest link in any system, but threats can be minimized.
- **User access levels** are used to limit the information that a user can access, read or edit. This may be limited to data that is relevant only to them or to protect personal information.
- **Passwords** are essential in preventing unauthorized access to a computer system, but they need to be complex enough so that they cannot be guessed or calculated by hackers.

What is a Strong Password?

- The security of any computer system, application or website is only as strong as the passwords used to access it.
- When creating a password, always follow these rules:
  - Make sure passwords are at least eight characters long.
  - Use upper- and lower-case characters.
  - Include special characters (for example ?, # and %).
  - Avoid real dictionary words.
  - Avoid any personal information, for example the names of family members, important dates, the names of pets and telephone numbers.
  - Regularly change any password and never use it for more than one system.

Key Point

'$1zZfpwn_@98' is a good password, whereas 'computer123' is not.

Quick Test

1. List three systems used at home that include encryption.
2. Why should a password never be used for more than one system?
3. Why might an organization use a hacker to carry out penetration testing?

Key Words

firewalls
anti-malware
encryption
public encryption key
private key
cypher
network policies
network forensics
penetration testing
user access levels
passwords

System Software

You must be able to:

- Describe the purpose and function of system software
- Explain the role of an operating system within a computer system
- Describe the various uses of utility and application software.

Why Do We Need an Operating System?

- The **operating system** (OS) is the link between the hardware, the software and the user, and it is essential to the function of any computer.
- The OS allows the user to access applications and allows the CPU to communicate with peripheral devices and system memory.
- All modern computer systems (for example smartphones, tablets, and portable and desktop computers) use an OS.

> **Key Point**
>
> No matter what size a modern computer is, it will have an OS.

Operating System Key Functions

- Modern OSs provide a **graphical user interface** (GUI) that allows ease of use without having to enter commands into a command line prompt. This includes the use of a mouse to select menus, and drag and drop file management.
- **User management** allows more than one user to log in to a system but with their own preferences and levels of functionality.
- The OS can perform multiple tasks simultaneously by managing and allocating the amount of resources and memory that the CPU and memory modules can use.
- Peripherals such as printers, scanners, graphics tablets and webcams will each run using specific **drivers** installed and regularly updated by the OS.
- **File management** allows users to organize their work into folders and subfolders with appropriate filenames.

Why is Utility Software Important?

- **Utility software** performs specialized tasks that support the OS.
- These may be included as part of the OS installation or may be additional **third-party applications**.
- Utility software functionality may relate to system security or to file and disk management.

What Tasks are Performed by Utility Software?

- Utility software, such as firewalls and anti-malware, performs security tasks to keep a system safe.
- Encryption software scrambles data into an unreadable form that cannot be read unless you have a specific key to decrypt it.
- **Defragmentation** software analyses data and how it is stored on a disk. It then rearranges the data into a more logical sequence to allow faster access.
- **Compression** software reduces the file size of documents and system files so that they take up less space on a disk.
- If a computer system fails or is damaged then a file backup is essential to restore files to their pre-damaged state.
  - Backup software regularly copies important files to an external storage device.
  - This can involve copying all important files in a **full backup** or an **incremental backup** (copying only the files that have changed since the previous backup).

Application Software

- The software installed into an OS to actually produce work is **application software**.
- This includes word processing, desktop publishing, data modelling and games applications.

> **Key Point**
>
> Utility software usually runs in the background, performing a useful service such as anti-virus protection.

> **Key Point**
>
> Like writing a letter, application software has a specific purpose.

> **Key Words**
>
> operating system
> graphical user interface
> user management
> drivers
> file management
> utility software
> third-party applications
> defragmentation
> compression
> full backup
> incremental backup
> application software

> **Quick Test**
>
> 1. Find examples of four OSs.
> 2. Why is an incremental backup more appropriate for a large computer system?
> 3. Look at the computer system you have access to. Can you divide the programs installed into application, utility and OS software?

Where space is not provided, write your answers on a separate piece of paper.

The Purpose and Function of the Central Processing Unit

1 Name the **three** common elements of all computer systems. [3]

2 A robotic arm in a manufacturing plant would be an _____ device. [1]

3 Which area of a CPU helps to prevent data bottlenecks? [1]

4 What does the abbreviation ALU stand for? [1]

5 What area of the CPU directs the flow of data around the system? [1]

6 What term is used to describe a physical pathway shared by signals to and from components of a computer system? [1]

7 What does the abbreviation MDR stand for? [1]

8 What is the purpose of the MDR? [1]

9 In which area of the von Neumann architecture is the accumulator found? [1]

10 Which area of the von Neumann architecture holds the memory location address of the next piece of data required? [1]

Systems Architecture

1 In the fetch–decode–execute cycle, in which area is an instruction carried out? [1]

2 *The CPU has its own memory storage.* True or false? [1]

3 For the CPU to understand the instructions fetched from memory, they must be

.... [1]

4 Complete the paragraph below using the words from the box. [4]

| slower | very fast | more efficient | L1 cache |

.... is used to store very frequently accessed data. It is quite small but .... The L2 cache is .... and further away but still .... than the main memory.

5 Modern CPUs can have more than two levels of cache. True or false? [1]

6 What **three** characteristics define the performance of a CPU? [3]

7 How many cores do the following processors have?

a) 2-GHz hexa core. .... [1]

b) 3-GHz quad core. .... [1]

c) 2-GHz single core. .... [1]

d) 4-GHz dual core. .... [1]

e) 2-GHz octa core. .... [1]

8 Define the term 'embedded system'. **[2]**

9 The pump control of a dishwasher has a fault. What is an advantage of this being an embedded system? **[1]**

Memory

1 RAM is sometimes referred to as being like which of the following? Tick **one** box. **[1]**

A Our long-term memory. ☐ **B** Our short-term memory. ☐ **C** Our permanent memory. ☐

2 Name the **two** types of RAM. **[2]**

3 Which of RAM and ROM has the smaller storage capacity? _____ **[1]**

4 What feature of ROM allows instructions to be written to it when it is manufactured? **[1]**

5 Give **two** reasons why a CPU uses RAM rather than the computer hard drive for short-term calculations. **[2]**

6 Where is BIOS data stored? **[1]**

7 Is virtual memory created to support RAM or ROM? _____ **[1]**

8 Where is virtual memory created? **[1]**

9 List two improvements that flash memory has over traditional ROM chips. **[1]**

10 Why might manufacturers now use flash memory instead of ROM chips for the BIOS? **[1]**

11 Why do some smartphones allow SD cards to be used to expand on-board memory? **[2]**

Storage Types, Devices and Characteristics

1 Secondary storage refers to storage not contained within which **two** computer components? **[2]**

2 What does the abbreviation SSD stand for? **[1]**

3 How many bits make up 1 byte? **[1]**

4 A terabyte is how many megabytes? **[1]**

5 Match each prefix with its definition. **[4]**

kilo	million

mega	trillion

giga	thousand

tera	billion

6 What is the most common storage media for modern console games? **[1]**

7 Which type of storage has many complex moving parts? **[1]**

8 List **two** advantages and **two** disadvantages of optical storage. **[4]**

9 Name **three** types of optical disc. **[3]**

10 Why might replacing a magnetic hard drive in a laptop with an SSD make it run faster? **[1]**

11 Early portable MP3 players had small magnetic hard drives. What was a common problem with them? **[1]**

Where space is not provided, write your answers on a separate piece of paper.

Common System Threats

1 List **three** pieces of personal information desired by online criminals. **[3]**

2 Complete the paragraph below using the words from the box. **[5]**

| password | social network | bank | hacker | accounts |

Using the same _____ across systems, for example a _____ and

a_____, is dangerous. A _____ gaining access to one will have

access to many more of your _____.

3 Malware is short for _____. **[2]**

4 Which type of malware hides its true intention by pretending to be something else? **[1]**

5 A self-replicating form of malware is called a _____. **[1]**

6 What is the purpose of ransomware? **[2]**

7 List **three** current methods of phishing. **[3]**

8 What is shouldering? [2]

_____

_____

9 How is blagging different from other social engineering methods? [1]

_____

10 How does a brute force attack work? [2]

_____

_____

11 What does the abbreviation DoS stand for? [2]

_____

_____

12 Name **two** dangers of a poor network policy. [2]

_____

_____

Threat Prevention

1 Why must anti-malware be regularly updated? [1]

_____

2 Public and private keys are part of _____. [1]

3 Hardware or software designed to control the transmission of data is called a

_____. [1]

4 Match each term with its description. [3]

Network policies	Monitors and records network traffic in case of any network attacks.
Network forensics	Searching for potential weaknesses in a system that could be exploited.
Penetration testing	Rules all users within a large network must follow to protect security.

5 Why might two users in the same network have different access levels? [1]

6 What is normally the weakest link in any network? [1]

7 Which **two** of the following should not form part of a password? Tick the correct boxes. [2]

A Upper-case and lower-case characters. ☐

B Favourite pet names. ☐

C Special characters. ☐

D Telephone numbers. ☐

System Software

1 An operating system is the link between which **three** elements? [3]

2 What does the abbreviation GUI stand for? [1]

3 List **four** examples of computer peripherals. [4]

....

....

....

....

4 Drag and drop became possible with which device? [1]

....

5 If a device driver is not regularly updated, what may happen? [1]

....

6 Complete the paragraph below using the words from the box. [3]

| supports   system security   management |

Utility software .... the operating system, performing tasks such as

.... and disk ....

7 What is file compression? [1]

....

8 How does an incremental backup differ from a full backup? [1]

....

9 What is the rearranging of files to speed up access and reduce size called? [1]

....

10 List **three** types of application software. [3]

....

....

....

Wired and Wireless Networks 1

You must be able to:

- Explain the difference between wired and wireless networks
- Describe different types of network.

How are Networks Formed?

- Linking together computer devices so that they can communicate and exchange information is what forms a **network**.
- Desktops, laptops, tablets, printers, smart TVs and smartphones can all connect to a network, and the Internet is built on many networks connected using cables and wireless technology.

Local Area Network

- A local area network (**LAN**) consists of computers and peripheral devices connected in a single or local area such as a school or an office building.
- Each computer or device can run independently but can exchange information through switches.

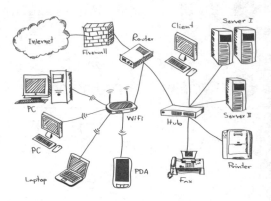

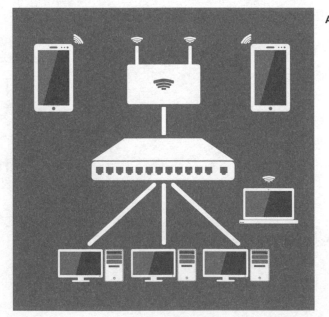

A LAN

Wide Area Network

- Connecting one LAN to another, or multiple LANs over a large distance, forms a wide area network (**WAN**).
- A WAN may span across the globe using telephone lines, fibre-optic undersea cables and even satellites.
- The largest WAN today is the Internet.

Key Point

Connecting multiple LANs together forms a WAN.

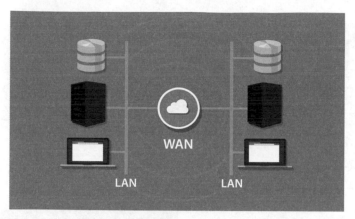

A WAN

WAN

LAN   LAN

What Affects the Performance of a Network?

- **Bandwidth**, measured in bits per second, is the amount of data that can pass between two network devices per second.
- There are several factors that can affect the performance, and potential bandwidth speed, of a network:
  - The quality of the transmission media, either wired or wireless.
  - There can be interference from external factors, such as distance, and other electronic devices, such as microwaves.
  - The bandwidth must be shared between all of the users of the same network, lowering everyone's connection speed.

Bandwidth

ENTER

What is a Client–Server Network?

- A client–server network is when a main computer **server** (that controls access and hosts programs) is accessed from multiple **client** computers.
- This means that client machines can be relatively low specification, as most of the processing workload, security, user access and backups can be carried out by the central server.

What is a Peer-to-Peer Network?

- All computers within a peer-to-peer network act as both client and server – they share files, programs and network access.
- Security **permissions** are shared across the network, and a user can access the contents of any other user's computer on the same network.

Peer-to-peer

Key Words

LAN
WAN
bandwidth
server
client
permissions

Quick Test

1. Why would an international bank use a WAN?
2. What security issues may arise from connecting to a peer-to-peer network?
3. Name three factors that can slow down a network.

Wired and Wireless Networks 2

You must be able to:

- Describe the devices used to connect computers to a network
- Explain how networks link across the world, forming the Internet.

Network Hardware

- To create a LAN from stand-alone computers, the following hardware devices are required:
  - network interface controllers/cards (NICs)
  - network switches
  - routers
  - wireless access points
  - transmission media.
- **NICs** plug directly into the motherboard of a desktop computer and allow the computer to communicate with a network using either an Ethernet cable or wireless technology.
  - Each NIC includes a **media access control** (MAC) address that provides a unique identifier within a LAN.
  - In newer computers and laptops, NIC functionality is usually built into the motherboard rather than on a separate card.
- **Network switches** act as a gateway between computers, allowing information to be passed between them and sent directly to a specified destination MAC address.
- **Routers** connect networks together. This connection may be between multiple LANs to create a WAN or between a LAN and the Internet (which is a much larger network).
- **Wireless access points** are devices that connect to a network and allow external wireless devices, such as smartphones, laptops and tablets, to connect to that network.
- **Transmission media** is the term used to describe how network devices are connected to each other, using either cables or wireless communication.
  - Wired networks traditionally use copper wire Ethernet cables to transmit data between devices, up to a maximum of 100 metres.
  - More recently, fibre-optic cables (which transmit data as flashes of light) have been used for larger networks requiring bigger bandwidths over longer distances.
  - Wireless technology (often referred to as Wi-Fi) uses radio waves to transmit data between compatible routers and computers.
  - Wireless networks also include 3G and 4G mobile phone networks and Bluetooth.

> ### Key Point
>
> Every network-compatible device has a permanent MAC address to identify it on a network.

Global Networks and the Internet

- The Internet that we know and use today is a vast interconnected collection of all of the network technologies described in this chapter.
- The World Wide Web (WWW), proposed by Tim Berners-Lee in 1990, utilizes this technology to publish pages written in HyperText Markup Language (HTML), which can be viewed using a web browser anywhere in the world.
- The **Domain Name Server** (or Service) (DNS) is an Internet naming service that links the **Internet Protocol** (IP) address of a computer on a network to a text-based website address that is easier to remember, for example www.collins.co.uk.
- **Hosting** means allowing users to access a specific computer – the host – via a network connection.
  - The host may be an individual computer or a server anywhere in the world – it must be constantly running and maintained so that users can always access it.
  - Web-hosting companies follow this process on a much larger scale, renting space on their network for individuals and organizations to host their own websites.
  - It is possible to run a hosting computer at home, but a high level of technical knowledge is required.
- **Cloud computing** allows Internet users not only to access remote files but also to run applications.
  - Multiple users can access workplace applications such as word processors, graphics software and even games directly from a remote server without the need to install them on their own computer.
  - This allows users to access the latest software from any Internet-connected location and provides opportunities for collaboration and remote working.

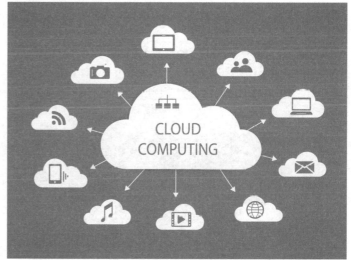

What is a Virtual Network?

- A **virtual network** is created using software rather than physical devices.
- Virtual LANs can be created within a large LAN to allow groups of specific users to share data without the need for additional physical servers and switches.

Quick Test

1. What device is required to connect LANs together as a WAN?
2. What service links IP addresses and website names?
3. List five uses of cloud computing.

Key Words
media access control
switches
routers
Domain Name Server
Internet Protocol
hosting
cloud computing
virtual network

Network Topologies

You must be able to:

- Explain the term 'network topology'
- Describe star and mesh topologies.

What is a Network Topology?

- A **network topology** is the arrangement of computers and network devices in either a physical or a logical topographical structure.
- There are many configurations, each with associated advantages and disadvantages.
- These include star, mesh, bus and ring topologies.
- Network-compatible technology includes routers and switches, desktop computers, laptops, printers, smartphones, tablets and storage devices.
- Each device at an intersection/connection point is referred to as a node.

Key Point

A **node** is any device connected within a network.

Connecting Computers in a Star Topology

- At the centre of a **star network** is a server.
- Each compatible device has its own connection to the server.
- The server directs data transmissions between devices on the network.

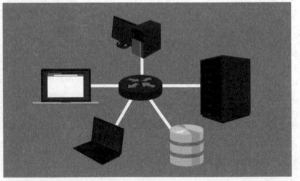

A Star Topology

Advantages and Disadvantages

Advantages	Disadvantages
• The failure of one device, as long as it is not the server, will not affect the rest of the network. • The network can be expanded by adding devices until the server capacity is reached. • Localized problems can be identified quickly. • Data can be directed to a specific address via the central server – this reduces network traffic.	• If the server fails, then the whole network will collapse. • Extensive cabling and technical knowledge is needed to maintain the server.

Connecting Computers in a Mesh Topology

- In a **mesh network**, every device within the network is connected to every other device.
- Network traffic is shared between all devices.

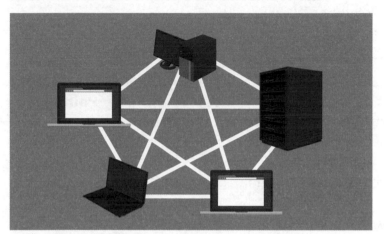

A Mesh Topology

Advantages and Disadvantages

Advantages	Disadvantages
• All devices share the network load, helping the network to run smoothly. • If one device fails, the network will continue to run, as all of the devices are connected to all of the other devices. • Adding more devices will not affect the speed of the network.	• Managing the network requires a high level of network expertise. • The network can be expensive to set up because of the number of devices required.

Additional Network Topologies

- As well as star and mesh, there are many other network topologies, for example a bus network and a ring network.
- A **bus network** has a central spine of network cabling.
  - Advantage – it is often used in small or temporary networks.
  - Disadvantages – its performance is affected by load, and if the spine fails then so does the whole network.
- A **ring network** has all computers connected in a circle. Data is transmitted around the circle until it reaches its destination.
  - Advantage – data travels quickly, in one direction.
  - Disadvantage – if one node fails, then the whole network fails.

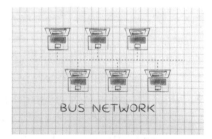

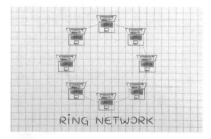

Quick Test

1. How are devices connected in a mesh network?
2. What happens if the server fails in a star network?
3. Give four examples of a network node.

Key Words

topology
star network
mesh network

Protocols and Layers

You must be able to:

- Explain Wi-Fi connectivity and its need for encryption
- Describe network protocols, including the term 'Ethernet' and the concept of layers
- Describe why IP and MAC addresses are used
- Describe packet switching.

Wi-Fi Technology

- Compatible devices must contain a **Wi-Fi-certified** chip to connect to a wireless LAN (WLAN) broadcast signal between 2.4 and 5 GHz.
- Each frequency range is divided into channels. Using channels with slightly different frequencies means that devices can run on the same network without interference and signal loss.
- External users connecting to a WLAN without a cable raises security concerns. Most Wi-Fi networks, therefore, are encrypted and require a user to enter a password to connect.
- Current Wi-Fi encryption standards include:
  - **Wired Equivalent Privacy** (WEP) – the oldest and least secure standard. It can be easily hacked and is not recommended for modern devices.
  - **Wi-Fi-Protected Access** (WPA and, more recently, WPA2) – uses modern encryption methods combined with a secure password to protect WLAN access.

The Concept of Network Addresses

- A MAC address (for example 583D8F87A6B2):
  - is hardwired into network devices and is used within a LAN when sending and receiving data
  - is normally stored in hexadecimal format.
- IP addresses (for example 172.16.1.40):
  - are assigned to network devices to allow data transfer across the Internet using the Transmission Control Protocol (TCP)/IP
  - are described as **static** if permanently assigned to a computer, often an important specific computer or server, by an Internet service provider
  - are described as **dynamic** if assigned by the router within a network and can change each time the network is restarted
  - are normally stored as four denary numbers.

Network Protocols

- Networks are built using multiple devices from manufacturers all around the world.
- For them to communicate effectively they must follow rules (**protocols**).

> **Key Point**
>
> WLAN is short for wireless local area network.

There are 14 channels at 2.4 GHz, but only three of these (1, 6 and 11) do not overlap.

There are 25 channels at 5 GHz.

There are 24 non-overlapping channels.

Protocol	Description
Ethernet	The most common type of connecting cable in a LAN. Used to connect NICs, routers and switches, it can handle large amounts of data, up to 100 gigabits per second (Gbit s^{-1}). Modern variations include Cat 5 and Cat 6, using twisted pairs of wire.
TCP/IP	A set of protocols that allow computers on multiple networks, including the Internet, to transmit and receive data packets.
HTTP (Hypertext Transfer Protocol)	Rules followed by web servers and web clients, or browsers, which host and present websites based on our requests.
HTTPS (HTTP Secure)	HTTP Secure encrypts communication between server and client. This makes secure online shopping and banking possible.
FTP (File Transfer Protocol)	Used to connect clients and servers across a network to exchange files. Traditionally used to upload files to a web server.
POP (Post Office Protocol)	Used to log in to and retrieve email messages from a mail server. When connected, all messages are downloaded to that device.
IMAP (Internet Message Action Protocol)	Allows access to an email server but, rather than downloading messages, they are simply read. This allows synchronized access from multiple devices, unlike POP.
SMTP (Simple Mail Transfer Protocol)	Used to send email messages to an email server rather than to receive messages.

The Concept of Layers

- The term '**layers**' refers to a set of protocols with specific functions.
- Data can be transmitted between adjacent layers.

Layer Name	Description and Relevant Protocols
Application layer	Data relevant to web browsers and email clients – includes HTTP, FTP and SMTP.
Transport layer	Ensures that data is sent and received correctly between network hosts – includes TCP.
Internet (or network) layer	Communicates the IP addresses of all devices used in data traffic between network routers – includes IP.
Data link layer	Concerned with physical data transfer over cables – includes Ethernet.

What is Packet Switching?

- When data is transmitted across a network it is broken down into small pieces called packets, and then transmitted and reassembled at the destination.
- This is called **packet switching** and is used by routers to direct data packets across multiple networks.
    - It allows the most efficient route to be taken by each individual packet.
    - Even if each packet takes a different pathway, data can still be reassembled at the destination.
- Each packet contains the source and destination address, a portion of the data and a reference to how the packets fit back together.

Key Point

Without HTTPS, online transactions would not be secure.

Key Words

Wi-Fi certified
protocols
layers
packet switching

Quick Test

1. Which two layers is TCP/IP linked to?
2. Which email protocol would an online-based email service use?

Where space is not provided, write your answers on a separate piece of paper.

Common System Threats

1 Name **three** areas of our lives in which we are now often connected to networks. [3]

2 Your computer is infected with spyware. Describe **two** ways that the creator of the spyware may profit. [2]

3 What term describes the process of redirecting your browser to a fake version of a popular site? [1]

4 Deleting a user's document files or corrupting start-up files, preventing a computer from booting, is a possible symptom of a .... [1]

5 What is the purpose of adware? [2]

6 Impersonating a friend or a financial organization via a text message is an example of .... [1]

7 Why do computer scams often target the young and the elderly? [1]

8 Apart from at an ATM, give **two** examples of where shouldering might take place. [2]

9 Name **three** types of valuable information that can be collected using data interception and theft. [3]

10 Give **two** examples of demands often made following a denial of service attack. **[2]**

11 What does the abbreviation SQL stand for? _____ **[3]**

12 How does a SQL injection attack work? **[3]**

Threat Prevention

1 Name **three** pieces of malware that anti-malware is designed to stop. **[3]**

2 Which kind of firewall is more robust: hardware based or software based? **[1]**

3 Why do instant messaging systems use encryption? **[2]**

4 List **three** possible network policy areas. **[3]**

5 Why might an online auction site use penetration testing? **[2]**

6 Why might a portable USB drive be a risk to a large network? **[2]**

7 User access level may be linked to read/write file access. Explain the difference between read and write. **[2]**

8 Describe a potential problem with a long complex password. **[1]**

9 Which **two** of the following would be classed as a strong password? Tick the correct options. **[2]**

A $thfL98&2hgf ☐   D blue12345 ☐

B P@55word ☐   E QWERTY2017 ☐

C FFj32* ☐   F iTYf76v()-@qPL ☐

10 Why should a password be changed regularly? **[1]**

11 Why are users told to avoid using dictionary words in passwords? **[1]**

System Software

1 Name **three** devices that use operating systems. **[3]**

2 List **three** current operating systems. **[3]**

3 Before GUI systems, what was the standard for user access? **[1]**

4 Describe **two** key elements of a GUI system. [2]

_____

_____

5 What is OS user management? [1]

_____

6 How is user management beneficial? [2]

_____

_____

7 In relation to an OS, what is meant by third-party applications? [1]

_____

8 Why might a company use encryption software to encrypt its stored data? [1]

_____

9 If a computer system and its files becomes corrupted, how will backup software help? [2]

_____

_____

10 Name **three** storage devices that can be used for file backups. [3]

_____

_____

_____

11 Name **two** security-based utility software packages. [2]

_____

_____

12 Which of the following is not a definition of application software? Tick the correct option. [1]

   A Small programs used to run peripheral devices. ☐

   B Software used to produce practical work such as writing a letter. ☐

   C Software that constantly scans for malware. ☐

Where space is not provided, write your answers on a separate piece of paper.

Wired and Wireless Networks 1

1 List **five** network-compatible devices. [5]

2 What do the abbreviations LAN and WAN stand for? [2]

3 What is often referred to as the largest WAN today? [1]

4 The performance of a network can be affected by several elements. Name **three** of these elements. [3]

5 Describe a client–server network. [3]

6 A popular network for sharing media across the Internet is called a _____. [1]

7 Bandwidth is measured in _____. [1]

8 Describe a common security concern of using peer-to-peer networks. [1]

9 Undersea network cables usually use which type of technology? [1]

Wired and Wireless Networks 2

1 The abbreviation NIC stands for .... [1]

2 List **three** types of wireless connectivity. [3]

   ....

   ....

   ....

3 What device is normally used to connect LANs together? [1]

   ....

4 What does the abbreviation MAC stand for? [1]

   ....

5 Name the service linking an IP address and a website address. [1]

   ....

6 A software-based group of computers within an existing network is referred to as a

   .... [1]

7 Complete the following paragraph using the words in the box. [4]

cloud computing	Internet	remote	applications

   .... allows .... users not only to access

   .... files but also to run .... such as word processors,

   graphics software and even games.

8 Which programming language is commonly used to create web pages? [1]

   ....

9 Briefly describe the process of commercial web hosting. [2]

   ....

   ....

Computer Networking

Practice Questions

Network Topologies

1 List **four** network topologies. **[4]**

....

....

2 What device would normally be at the centre of a star network? **[1]**

....

3 Describe **two** advantages and **two** disadvantages of a star network. **[4]**

....

....

....

....

4 *If a device fails in a mesh network, the network will fail.* True or false? **[1]**

....

....

....

5 What is a potential problem of a ring network? **[1]**

....

6 Which topology has a central spine of network cabling? **[1]**

....

7 Why would a mesh network require more cabling than a star network? **[1]**

....

8 Describe the term 'node'. **[1]**

....

Protocols and Layers

1 What are the **two** common frequencies for Wi-Fi networks? **[2]**

2 Why is WEP not currently recommended for use? **[2]**

3 List **three** network protocols. **[3]**

4 Name the term used to describe how routers direct data packets across multiple networks. **[1]**

5 Which protocol allows secure online shopping to take place? **[1]**

6 Uploading files to a web server would use which protocol? **[1]**

7 Match each term with its description. **[4]**

Application layer	Concerned with physical data transfer over cables.
Transport layer	Communicates the IP addresses of devices between routers.
Internet (or network) layer	Data relevant to web browsers and email clients.
Data link layer	Ensures that data is correctly sent and received between network hosts.

8 Cat 5 and Cat 6 are common types of _____. **[1]**

9 What do the abbreviations TCP/IP stand for? **[1]**

Ethical and Legal Concerns

You must be able to:

- Describe ethical concerns surrounding privacy, security and automation
- Describe legal issues arising as a result of increased use of computer technology.

Ethical Use

- The **ethical use** of computer technology means trying to cause no harm to others and acting in a morally responsible way to improve society.
- This applies to our own use of technology and to how others treat us.

Maintaining Our Privacy

GPS technology

- Our increased use of technology, for example smartphones, social networking and Internet-connected devices, means that our actions are often recorded without us knowing it. Examples of this include:
  - Mobile phone service providers know our location through **Global Positioning System** (GPS) technology and mobile signal triangulation; they also know the people we contact and the mobile applications we use.
  - Websites track our search history using **cookies** and provide it to others.
  - Social networks routinely ask for personal information and like us to post it online.
  - Internet service providers log our search histories and browsing data.
  - **Streaming services** log our music and video choices.

> **Key Point**
>
> Cookies store personal information about your browsing history.

Security Concerns

- With so much data being gathered about us and our daily actions, many questions are being raised about how much of this information should be accessible.

- Should mobile phones and Internet search records be routinely checked by government agencies for evidence of malicious intent, such as planning an act of terrorism?
- What are social networks doing with all of the data they hold about us?
- Should our own access be restricted to prevent us accessing harmful information? Who should regulate this?

Are We Being Replaced?

- Robots and automated devices are ideal for situations that may be dangerous to humans or for jobs that are extremely repetitive:
  - Pilotless drones are now used routinely in military conflicts.
  - Robots are used to disable explosive devices and to enter poisonous environments.
  - Car manufacturing has been revolutionized by robots, carrying out repetitive tasks 24 hours a day, replicating the same movement exactly each time.
- But what happens to those individuals who are replaced?

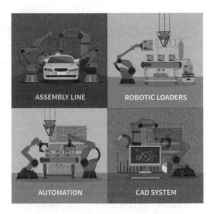

New Opportunities for Crime

- The way that we interact with technology has increased our legal impact on society through online communication, and has created new opportunities for criminals.
- Criminals selling illegal products and services online have found customers around the world via the Internet (this kind of activity used to be limited to shady back-alley deals).
- Hackers use a variety of methods to either access our accounts or discover personal information that will facilitate further crime.
- Government agencies struggle to keep up with the pace of computer crime.

Am I Breaking the Law?

- The vast amount of information available online also means that it is not always obvious when laws are broken. Users can quickly find films, music and games to download that break copyright laws.
- People can buy products from around the world, and have them delivered to their homes, without knowing the source of the product or whether it meets safety regulations.

> **Quick Test**
>
> 1. Describe three ways that we share our private information online.
> 2. Describe three positive uses of drone technology.
> 3. What are the dangers of unregulated streaming services?

Key Words

Global Positioning System
cookies
streaming services

Cultural and Environmental Concerns

You must be able to:

- Discuss the cultural impact of computer technology on our daily lives
- Describe the term 'digital divide' and how it came about
- Describe the environmental impact of computer technology on energy use and materials.

How our Lives are Changing

- Communication now includes text, picture and video messaging from any location in the world to another.
- We use social networks and **blogs** to publish our thoughts worldwide and we can contact directly on our smartphones the politicians and entertainment stars whom we read about!
- **Medical** advances include full-body scanners and smart watches that monitor our body and transmit the data online. Computer simulations analyse biological viruses and model new medicines.
- **Transport** technology is developing to automate not only the traffic lights and signals that we follow but also the vehicles that we use. Computer management systems control traditional motor vehicles, the latest electric-powered versions and the many driverless car prototypes now in production.
- **Educational** content now spans the world, and students who are able to get online can access not only local resources but also lessons delivered on almost any subject via video streaming services. The equipment used in classrooms also includes interactive whiteboards and **multimedia** systems.
- Many **leisure** activities, from **immersive** video gaming to three-dimensional cinema screens, use the latest computer-generated imagery (CGI). Streaming media services run complex algorithms to provide what they think we would like.
- The ability to not only find new jobs but also run an entire business online has completely changed the **employment** market.

What is the Digital Divide?

- The increased access to technology is not consistent across the world or even within countries.
- Many countries/areas are limited by financial or geographical constraints, and broadband Internet connections are not yet available everywhere.

> ### Key Point
>
> The **digital divide** is the social and economic gap between those who have and those who do not have access to computer technology.

- This lack of access can then expand the divide further. For example:
  - Some jobs are advertised initially (or only) online.
  - Customers can usually find the cheapest products and household services through the Internet.

The Impact on the Environment

- Developments in computer science affect our environment in both positive and negative ways.

Positive	Negative
Reductions in the use of paper.	Increased energy consumption of digital devices.
Replacement of physical media with downloads reduces material costs.	Increased greenhouse gas emissions to meet additional power needs.
Mobile and home working reduces transportation costs.	Cost of the transportation of raw and synthetic materials for the production of smart devices.
Smarter devices control their energy usage to meet our needs – this reduces wastage.	It is difficult to recycle waste materials from outdated or unwanted technology.
The development of increasingly efficient renewable energy sources.	Devices often include toxic materials.

 E-WASTE

Quick Test

1. List three ways that recycling old computers can help the environment.
2. What are some of the concerns about driverless cars?
3. Research five rare elements currently used in the production of a smartphone.

Key Words

blogs
multimedia
immersive

Computer Science Legislation

You must be able to:

- Describe the reasons for and key concepts behind the following: the Data Protection Act 1998, the Computer Misuse Act 1990, the Copyright, Designs and Patents Act 1988, Creative Commons Licensing and the Freedom of Information Act 2000
- Understand the difference between open source and proprietary software.

Laws

- New laws exist to regulate our increased use of computer technology and to make sure that individuals and organizations can be held responsible for any misuse.

Data Protection Act 1998

- Created to protect the personal information held about individuals within organizations.
- Its main principles are:
  - Data should be fairly and lawfully processed.
  - Data must be obtained and used only for specified purposes.
  - Data shall be adequate, relevant and not excessive.
  - Data should be accurate and kept up to date.
  - Data should not be kept for longer than necessary.
  - Access must be granted to data subjects to enable them to check and correct their entries.
  - Data must be kept safe and secure.
  - Data should not be transferred outside the EEA (European Economic Area) to another country without adequate protection legislation.

Computer Misuse Act 1990

- Designed specifically to prevent hacking and the damage of computer systems by the following means:
  - intentional unauthorized access to programs or data that are not normally accessible
  - unauthorized access to material that could be used for further criminal activities
  - intentional damage to data or software using malware.

Copyright, Designs and Patents Act 1988

- Provides the creators of music, books, films and games with the right to control how their products are accessed and sold. This means that no one else has the right to copy or sell their work without permission.
- Using the Internet to access and download free copies of such **copyrighted** material is therefore illegal, as no money or credit will have passed to the original creator.

> ### Key Point
>
> Websites offering free streaming of the latest movies are breaking the Copyright, Designs and Patents Act 1988.

Creative Commons Licensing

- There are times when a creator will want to share their work but with conditions attached.
- The Creative Commons organization provides licences that allow people to use, share or edit pieces of work, depending on the licence given.
- The licences include:
  - public domain – no restrictions on use for any purpose
  - **attribution** – the original creator must be credited if the work is copied or used
  - attribution-non-commercial – work can be used only for non-commercial purposes.

Freedom of Information Act 2000

- This Act provides the public with a right to access information held by central and local governments.
- All requests must be considered but can be refused under certain circumstances.

Open Source and Proprietary Software

- **Open source** software is created to be shared openly online at no cost, with no limits on how it can be edited, copied or distributed.
  - Examples include Linux, GIMP (GNU Image Manipulation Programme) and Audacity.
- **Proprietary** software is owned by the individual or company who created it.
  - Permission to use the software is usually purchased through a licence, and the software cannot be edited or shared in any way.

Quick Test

1. Which act was specifically designed to prosecute hackers?
2. If a reporter would like to know how much a local council has spent on expenses, which act would apply?
3. Which act would prevent customer lists being sold to another business outside the EEA without permission?

Key Words

copyrighted
attribution
open source
proprietary

Where space is not provided, write your answers on a separate piece of paper.

Wired and Wireless Networks 1

1 State **two** reasons why a smart TV would have network access. **[2]**

2 Name a network device used to share information between other devices. **[1]**

3 *A WAN can link a maximum of two LANs.* True or false? **[1]**

4 A classroom has been provided with a set of low-specification computers. What network type would be best suited for using the computers effectively? **[1]**

5 Name **one** household kitchen device that can cause wireless network interference. **[1]**

6 Describe **two** benefits of the client–server network. **[2]**

7 Describe a potential benefit of connecting schools across the world using a WAN. **[1]**

8 A peer-to-peer network often shares security permissions. What does this mean? **[1]**

Wired and Wireless Networks 2

1 Complete the paragraph below using the words from the box. [2]

router	switch

A _____ connects compatible devices together and allows data to be shared,

creating a network. A _____ connects different networks together.

2 *Modern computers often have an integrated NIC, meaning that an additional card is not required.* True or false? [1]

_____

3 What device is often used to extend the range of a wireless network? [1]

_____

4 What type of limited-range wireless connectivity is often used for computer peripherals such as speakers and controllers? [1]

_____

5 In which decade did web pages first appear in the format we now recognize? [1]

_____

6 What device is required to connect an existing LAN to the Internet? [1]

_____

7 What is a main benefit of fibre-optic technology over traditional Ethernet cables? [1]

_____

8 Describe **two** potential problems that a small business could face if it uses only cloud computing. [2]

_____

_____

9 How does the DNS system help users browse the Internet? [1]

_____

Network Topologies

1 The sharing of network traffic between all devices is a benefit of which network topology? **[1]**

2 Name the topology that allows direct access between the server and each device. **[1]**

3 Which of the following would not normally be part of a network topology? Tick **one** box. **[1]**

A Laptop ☐

B Router ☐

C Server ☐

D Digital camera ☐

E Printer ☐

4 Match each topology with its potential problem. **[4]**

Star	Data travels quickly, in one direction, but if one node fails the network fails.
Mesh	If the central spine fails then so does the network.
Ring	If the server fails then the whole network will collapse.
Bus	Managing the network requires a high level of network expertise.

5 State the device needed to connect one star network to another star network. **[1]**

Protocols and Layers

1 What is the benefit of using non-overlapping Wi-Fi channels? [1]

2 How many channels are available at 2.4 GHz and at 5 GHz? [2]

3 What is the latest and most secure Wi-Fi encryption standard? [1]

4 In what format is a MAC address normally represented? [1]

5 192.168.1.2 is a typical .... [1]

6 Which email protocol is particularly suited to web-based email accounts? [1]

7 Which layer contains the HTTP, FTP and SMTP protocols? [1]

8 When purchasing devices to connect to a home wireless network, what identification mark should be looked for? [1]

9 Why is packet switching more efficient than transmitting whole data files? [2]

10 Describe the difference between a static IP address and a dynamic IP address. [2]

Where space is not provided, write your answers on a separate piece of paper.

Ethical and Legal Concerns

1 What does the abbreviation GPS stand for? _____ [1]

2 What are cookies and what do they contain? [2]

3 Describe **three** Internet security and privacy concerns. [3]

4 Describe **two** benefits of robotic car manufacturing. [2]

5 Give **two** reasons why selling illegal products online is appealing to criminals. [2]

6 What laws do Internet users often break without realizing? [1]

7 Identify **one** reason that government agencies access our online communications. [1]

8 How can access to a user's Internet history prevent cyberbullying? [1]

9 Identify **one** fun, **one** commercial and **one** government use for drones. [3]

....

....

....

10 Describe **two** advantages of using robots instead of humans in automated manufacturing. [2]

....

....

11 Why are hackers interested in our social network pages? [2]

....

....

Cultural and Environmental Concerns

1 List **three** areas of our lives that are being changed by technology. [3]

....

....

....

2 Identify **two** contributions to the digital divide. [2]

....

....

3 Complete the following table by placing a tick in **one** of the columns for each impact to indicate if it is positive or negative. [3]

Impact	Positive	Negative
Replacement of physical media with downloads.		
Cost of the transportation of raw and synthetic materials for the production of smart devices.		
The development of renewable energy sources.		

4 Describe **one** major benefit of online educational material.   [1]

_____

5 Why are smartphones often difficult to recycle?   [1]

_____

_____

6 Describe **one** potential benefit and **one** potential drawback of driverless cars.   [2]

_____

_____

7 Define the term 'immersive gaming'.   [1]

_____

_____

8 Why might a family's access to the Internet be limited by geographic constraints?   [1]

_____

9 Describe two benefits of moving towards a paperless office.   [1]

_____

Computer Science Legislation

1 State **three** principles of the Data Protection Act 1998.   [3]

_____

_____

_____

2 'Public domain' and 'attribution' are common terms in which set of guidelines?   [1]

_____

3 Some pieces of music and text are in the public domain.
What does the term 'public domain' mean? [1]

4 Websites that offer the latest cinema releases to stream for free are breaking which Act? [1]

5 The Computer Misuse Act 1990 targets which particular computer crime? [1]

6 *Open source software is owned by the company that created it and cannot be used without permission.*

True or false? [1]

7 Which Act allows an individual to request that an organization provides all details held about them? [1]

8 What is a data subject, as referred to in the Data Protection Act 1998? [1]

9 Intentional damage using malware is a crime according to which act? [1]

10 The term 'attribution' is often found in licensing Acts. What does it mean? [1]

11 *All Freedom of Information requests must be considered but can be refused under certain circumstances.*

True or false? [1]

Algorithms and Flow Diagrams

You must be able to:

- Understand the term 'algorithm' and its relationship with computer science
- Explain the term 'computational thinking'
- Describe searching and sorting algorithms
- Represent an algorithm using flow diagrams.

What is an Algorithm?

- To us and to a computer, an **algorithm** is a sequence of step-by-step instructions to solve a problem or carry out a task. Real-life examples might include:
  - getting ready for school
  - making a sandwich
  - setting up a bank account.
- A computing algorithm will generally follow the sequence input–process–output and can be broken down using the following terms:
  - **Sequence** – tasks are carried out step by step in sequence.
  - **Iteration** – certain tasks are repeated until a certain condition is met.
  - **Selection** – a decision needs to be made before the next step can be carried out.

A sandwich algorithm could be written as:

1. Take two slices of bread from packet.
2. Take butter and filling from fridge.
3. Spread butter on bread with knife.
4. Add filling on top of one slice.
5. Place second slice on top.
6. Cut sandwich in two.
7. Eat sandwich!

What is Computational Thinking?

- The ability to solve problems in a structured, logical way is referred to as computational thinking and includes the following skills:

Decomposition	The process of breaking tasks into smaller tasks that are easier to understand and then solve.
Abstraction	The removal of unwanted or unnecessary information from a task. This allows focus and clarity when solving problems.
Pattern recognition	Being able to identify patterns in data and to build efficient algorithms to take advantage of them.

- Understanding these skills and being able to imagine a solution to a problem in a series of steps is known as algorithmic thinking.

 Key Point

Repeating an action in a program until a condition is met is called iteration.

Searching Algorithms

- Searching for information based on a given criterion is a common task for computer algorithms. Two common methods are binary search and linear search:

1. **Binary search** looks for a specific value in an ordered or sorted list by:
   - comparing it with the middle or median value and deciding if it is higher or lower
   - taking the half of the list that is higher or lower and once again finding and comparing it with the middle value
   - repeating this process is repeated until the specific value is found.

2. **Linear search** simply takes each value in a list, one at a time, and compares it with the value required. This is repeated until the correct value is found. This process can be very slow, especially with large data sets.

Sorting Algorithms

- Sorting data means that data is generally easier to search, and it allows for more efficient algorithms. Three common methods are:

Bubble sort	The first two values in a list are compared with each other and the larger is placed first in the list. Then the next pair of values is checked and their order in the list is swapped if required. This process is repeated until the values are listed in descending order.
Merge sort	Data is repeatedly split into halves until each list contains only one item. The items are then merged back together into the order required.
Insertion sort	Each item in an unordered list is examined in turn and compared with the previous items in the list. Higher values than those before them are left in the same position, but lower values are compared with each in turn until they can be inserted into the correct place. This process is repeated until all items have been examined and inserted into their correct position, in ascending order.

Flow Diagrams

- **Flow diagrams**, or flow charts, are used to visualize an algorithm and show clearly the flow of information.
- They are generally used to plan computer programs before any coding is written.

Standard Flow Chart Symbols　　　　**An Example Flow Chart**

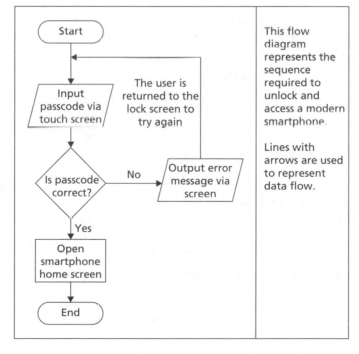

(rounded rectangle)	Used at the start or end point of a flow diagram.
(parallelogram)	Used to represent the input or output of data in a process.
(diamond)	Used when a decision or choice must be made.
(rectangle)	A process symbol, used to indicate a process or computational task being carried out.
(sub-routine box)	Used to represent a sub-routine that can be called at various points of an algorithm.

This flow diagram represents the sequence required to unlock and access a modern smartphone.

Lines with arrows are used to represent data flow.

Key Words

algorithm
sequence
iteration
selection
decomposition
abstraction
pattern
　recognition
binary search
linear search
bubble sort
merge sort
insertion sort
flow diagrams

Quick Test

1. Which type of search would be quickest with a large data set?
2. What process would be used to simplify a task by removing irrelevant information?

Pseudocode 1

You must be able to:

- Understand how pseudocode is used as a basic coding language
- Describe common pseudocode terms and keywords
- Write pseudocode to represent an algorithm.

What is Pseudocode?

- **Pseudocode** is a shared programming language that programmers use to plan and create a program before writing it in a specific coding language.
- Not designed to be understood directly by a computer, it uses terminology, syntax and structure common to most coding languages but in simple English.
- Simple mistakes that would halt a computer program, such as a bracket or quotation mark in the wrong place, are allowed in pseudocode.

Naming Conventions

- There are no fixed rules when it comes to naming variables or using keywords, but they must be consistent across multiple algorithms. The OCR examination board provides a pseudocode dictionary that gives examples of how coding will be presented in the examination and how the board would like student pseudocode to be written.
- An example of naming a variable or constant is using a capital letter to show a second word. Spaces should not be used, for example firstName or highScore.

Variables and Constants

- A **variable** is part of a program that can be assigned a specific value. It consists of a descriptive **identifier** and the value assigned to it. A variable can be changed within a program as it runs and is not fixed. For example:

  heightTree = 125

- A **constant** is a value that cannot be changed or edited within a running program.
- A constant also has an identifier. For example:

  daysofWeek = 7

Comments

- Adding personal notes to coding helps others to understand it and helps to explain your own thinking.
- Comments do not affect the running of the program and are denoted by //. For example:

  print("Hello, how can I help you?") // This line displays a welcome message

---

Common pseudocode keywords:

- **if** – used in a question, as part of a decision process
- **else** – used to provide a response if a statement is not met
- **then** – used to provide a response if a statement is met
- **while** – a loop with a condition set at the start
- **print** – used to display a response on screen to the user
- **input** – requires an entry from the user in response to a question
- **for** – used to create a counting loop.

> **Key Point**
>
> Remember that there are no fixed rules for pseudocode; it must just make sense.

 Please note that comments will be used in all of the following examples as guidance.

Print and Input

- The print command will display information, enclosed in quotation marks, on the screen to the user. The input command requires the user to type in a response to a question that can be processed in some way. For example:

```
name = input("Please type your name") // Question requires input
print("Hello", name) // Displays a hello message followed by the name
just typed in
```

Iteration and Selection

- Iteration is the act of repeating any process until a specified result is reached. For example:

```
for i = 0 to 9
    print("Good Morning")
next i // Good Morning will be printed 10 times (0–9 inclusive)
```

- A while loop can be used to repeat a question until a specific answer is provided. For example:

```
while x = "python"
x = input("Name a programming language beginning with P")
        do
                answer = input("Name a programming language beginning
with P")
        until answer == "python" // The loop will stop when python is
entered
```

- Selection allows decisions to be made within the program using if and else statements. Consider a true/false question for which the answer is false:

```
answer = input("Please answer True or False")
    if answer == "True" then
        print("Sorry, incorrect answer")
    clseif answer == "False" then
        print("Well done, correct answer") // Input is correct
    else
        print("Answer not recognized") // Shown if anything else is
entered
    endif
```

Key Point

Refer to OCR's website or specification for its current pseudocode dictionary.

Key Words

pseudocode
while
variable
identifier
constant

> **Quick Test**

1. What is iteration?
2. Provide three possible constants in a program.

Pseudocode 2

You must be able to:

- Understand the use of comparison operators
- Understand the use of arithmetic operators
- Understand the use of Boolean operators.

Comparison Operators

- Sometimes referred to as relational operators, **comparison operators** are used by programmers to test the relationship between two values.
- They are essential in writing programs that include logic questions, user input or the analysis of numerical data.

Operator	Function
==	Exactly equal to. The single = sign is used to assign a variable.
!=	Not equal to.
<	Less than.
<=	Less than or equal to.
>	Greater than.
>=	Greater than or equal to.

Arithmetic Operators

- Mathematical calculations in pseudocode make use of the functions in the following table.
- These operators may vary depending on the real programming language used when writing programs.

Operator	Function	Example
+	Addition of two or more values.	x = 10 + 5 x = 15
–	Subtraction of one value from another.	x = 20 – 10 x = 10
*	Multiplication of values.	x = 6 * 2 x = 12
/	One value divided by another.	x = 50 / 10 x = 5
MOD	**Modulus** – returns the remainder after a division.	x = 14MOD4 x = 2
DIV	**Quotient** – divides but returns only a whole number or integer.	x = 15DIV4 x = 3
^	**Exponentiation** – one value to the power of another.	x = 4^4 x = 256

Key Point

Note the differences between pseudocode used in an examination paper and real programming languages such as Python or JavaScript.

Boolean Operators

- **Boolean operators**, or logical operators, are used in programs to define relationships, using Boolean logic, between data values.

Operator	Function	Example
AND	If two or more statements are true.	if 10>5 **AND** 5>2 (both are true)
OR	If either statement is true.	if 10==5 **OR** 10>5 (10>5 is true)
NOT	To reverse the logical results of a statement.	if **NOT**(5>10) (result is true)

Quick Test

1. Why are two equals signs used rather than one when using comparison operators?
2. If x = 20MOD6, what would be the result?
3. If NOT(3 == 3), would the result be true or false?

Key Words

modulus
quotient
exponentiation
Boolean operators

Computational Logic

You must be able to:

- Explain the operations AND, OR and NOT
- Describe and create simple logic diagrams
- Represent logic diagrams using truth tables.

AND, OR and NOT

- Computer data is represented by a stream of binary data (0s and 1s).
- **Transistors** in a computer control the current flowing through it (off and on, 0 and 1), and the combination of multiple logic circuits using these two conditions allows more complex programs to be written.
- The operations AND, OR and NOT can be represented by **logic diagrams** or gates.
- Below each gate in the following diagram is a **truth table** representing potential inputs and outputs.

AND Gate

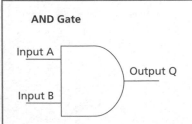

Input A
Input B
Output Q

Inputs		Output
A	**B**	**Q**
0	0	0
1	0	0
0	1	0
1	1	1

OR Gate

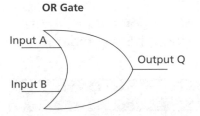

Input A
Input B
Output Q

Inputs		Output
A	**B**	**Q**
0	0	0
1	0	1
0	1	1
1	1	1

NOT Gate

Input A
Output Q

Inputs	Output
A	**Q**
0	1
1	0

Combining Logic Diagrams

- Adding together two or more gates allows more complex scenarios to be modelled. Consider the following scenarios:

Key Point

Truth tables represent binary inputs and outputs in the form of 0s and 1s.

Scenario 1:

Imagine a car on a fairground ride. On by default, a powerful lock P holds the car in place. It will not turn off, releasing the car, until the seat belt A AND the safety gate B are in place.

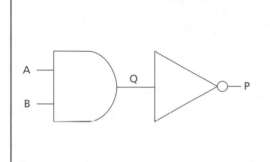

Inputs		Output	Output
A	B	Q	P
0	0	0	1
1	0	0	1
0	1	0	1
1	1	1	0

Scenario 2:

Imagine a security alarm circuit, which is set and running correctly when X is on. For this to happen, either of the alarm panels at B or C can be activated AND the door at A must be closed, deactivating a sensor.

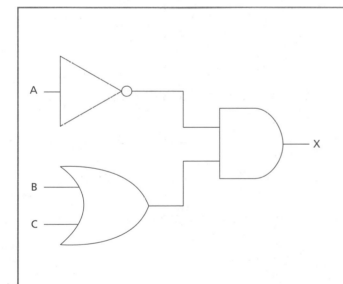

Inputs			Output
A	B	C	X
0	0	0	0
0	0	1	1
0	1	0	1
0	1	1	1
1	0	0	0
1	0	1	0
1	1	0	0
1	1	1	0

Quick Test

1. If a gate has two inputs and operates when either is on, which type of gate is it?
2. Which gate reverses the input signal?
3. How many potential inputs would a three-input gate have?

Key Words

transistors
logic diagrams
truth table

Where space is not provided, write your answers on a separate piece of paper.

Ethical and Legal Concerns

1 Describe the term 'ethical use'. [2]

2 Mobile smartphone applications use GPS. Why is this? [1]

3 Why should we be concerned if an application asks for permission to access our contact details? [1]

4 State **one** positive and **one** negative impact on employment of the use of robots in manufacturing. [2]

5 Computer criminals are constantly experimenting with new ways to commit electronic crime. What problem does this cause for government agencies working to prevent crimes happening? [1]

6 Why do young people often break copyright laws online without realizing? [2]

7 State **two** reasons why some people think that our Internet access should be filtered and controlled. [2]

Cultural and Environmental Concerns

1 Identify **one** positive and **one** negative aspect of online job applications. **[2]**

2 State **three** positive impacts on the environment of computer technology. **[3]**

3 Why are older members of society victims of the digital divide? **[1]**

4 What **two** factors will prevent a remote village from receiving the benefits of computer technology? **[2]**

5 What is e-waste? **[1]**

6 How can video streaming help teachers in rural areas? **[1]**

7 What piece of technology is often linked to immersive gaming? **[1]**

8 Why does the need for the 'latest gadget' have a negative impact on the environment? [2]

9 How might online communication improve a medical diagnosis? [1]

Computer Science Legislation

1 Match each issue with its related law. [3]

A request is made to a government minister about their expenses.	Computer Misuse Act 1990
An employee takes a company's customer database to a new company.	Freedom of Information Act 2000
An online email server is hacked and personal messages are stolen.	Data Protection Act 1998

2 What is the core principle of Creative Commons Licensing? [1]

3 What is the difference between open source software and proprietary software? [2]

4 List **four** types of copyright media that are often shared illegally online. [4]

5 In relation to Creative Commons Licensing, what does 'attribution-non-commercial' mean? **[2]**

6 Trying to access computer programs or data that are not normally publicly available is a crime under which law? **[1]**

7 A family keeps receiving bills addressed to the previous owners of their home. Why should the Data Protection Act 1998 prevent this? **[2]**

8 A new business has found images online that it would like to use for its new website. What should it do to stay within the law? **[2]**

Where space is not provided, write your answers on a separate piece of paper.

Algorithms and Flow Diagrams

1 Define the term 'algorithm'. [2]

Set of instructions

2 Match each term with its definition. [3]

Sequence	1	3	A decision needs to be made before the next step can be carried out.
Iteration	2	1	Tasks are carried out step by step in sequence.
Selection	3	2	Certain tasks are repeated until a certain condition is met.

3 State **three** key aspects of computational thinking. [3]

4 Which of binary search and linear search is considered slower with large files, and why? [2]

linear. Target may be at the end of thousands of records.

5 Describe briefly how a bubble sort works. [3]

6 Name **two** other methods of sorting data in addition to the bubble sort. [2]

merge sort, insertion sort

7 What shape is usually used to represent a decision in a flow diagram? [1]

diamond

8 Provide a description of each of the following flow chart symbols. [5]

Shape	(rounded rectangle)	(parallelogram)	(diamond)	(rectangle)	(rectangle with side bars)
Description	*Start/end*	*Output*	*Decision*		

Pseudocode 1

1 State **two** reasons why pseudocode rather than a specific language is used to plan programs. **[2]**

Easy to understand

2 Match each common pseudocode keyword with its definition. **[7]**

if	1		To display a response on screen to the user. 5
else	2		To provide a response if a statement is not met.
then	3		Requires an entry from the user in response to a question. 6
while	4		To provide a response if a statement is met. 3
print	5		Used in a question, as part of a decision process. 1
input	6		Used to create a counting loop. 7
for	7		A loop with a condition set at the start. 4

3 Why is it important to be consistent with naming conventions in pseudocode? **[1]**

4 Complete the following table by placing a tick in **one** of the columns for each value to indicate whether it is a variable or a constant. **[4]**

Value	Variable	Constant
numberCars = 19	✓	
daysofYear = 365		✓
hoursinDay = 24		✓
penWidth = 5	✓	

5 Why are comments used in pseudocode? **[1]**

6 Write a simple algorithm in pseudocode that asks the user their favourite colour and then agrees with their choice, quoting the colour in the response. **[2]**

7 Write a simple program that keeps asking how many days there are in a week until the correct answer is given. **[4]**

Pseudocode 2

1 Define the following pseudocode comparison operators.

    a) == _equal to_ [1]

    b) != _not equal to_ [1]

    c) < _less than_ [1]

    d) <= _less than or equal to_ [1]

    e) > _more than_ [1]

    f) >= _more than or equal to_ [1]

2 Which arithmetic operator returns the remainder after a division? [1]

MOD

3 What does the symbol '^' in 3^3 represent, and what would the answer be? [2]

indices, 3^3 = 9

4 Give **three** Boolean operators. [3]

AND, NOT, OR

5 How is the quotient function represented as an arithmetic operator? [1]

6 Find the value of x in the following statements.

    a) x = 6 * 4 _24_ [1]

    b) x = 3^6 _729_ [1]

    c) x = 9DIV5 _2_ [1]

    d) x = 21MOD10 _1_ [1]

7 Write a brief pseudocode program that asks what the temperature is outside. If the result falls between a value of 15 and a value of 25 then reply "Perfect!"; otherwise, reply "Not quite right". [4]

Computational Logic

1 What electronic component can control the flow of electricity? **[1]**

Diode

2 Name the **three** types of gates shown in the following diagram. **[3]**

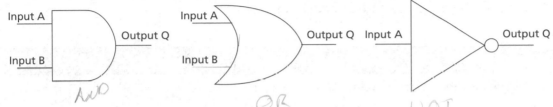

AND   OR   NOT

3 Complete the following OR gate truth table. **[4]**

Inputs		Output
A	**B**	**Q**
0	0	0
1	0	1
0	1	1
1	1	1

4 Create a logic diagram and truth table for each of the following scenarios.

a) A car (X) will not start until both doors (A AND B) and the boot (C) are closed. **[8]**

b) A water pump (X) will start if a water level sensor (A) deactivates OR if two switches (B AND C) are simultaneously pressed. **[8]**

5 Complete the truth table for the following logic diagram. **[8]**

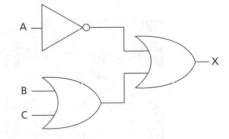

Inputs			Output
A	**B**	**C**	**X**
1		1	1
1	1	0	0

Programming Techniques 1

You must be able to:

- Explain common programming data types
- Use basic string manipulation
- Use basic file handling operations.

Data Types

- Categorizing data allows a computer to treat each data type differently.

Data Type	Description	Examples	Pseudocode
Integer	A whole number with no decimal point.	4, 10, –20	int
Boolean	Digital data – can present only two values.	1/0, yes/no, true/false, on/off	bool
Real (or float)	All numbers, including those with a decimal point.	1.435, 0.01, –3.5	real (or float)
Character	A single letter, number or symbol.	T, £, @	char
String	A collection of **alphanumeric** data characters and symbols. Usually enclosed in quotation marks.	"Grace", "15-12-14", "Am@ze1"	str

- **Casting**, or typecasting, is the conversion of one data type into another, for example converting a string into an integer or a real number or converting a number into a string:

```
int("17") // This converts string 17 into an integer
str(125) // This converts a number into a string
```

Key Point

Real numbers are often referred to as floats.

String Manipulation

- Normally written within quotation marks, a string is a collection of characters. Strings are often used in program inputs and outputs. For example:

```
string1 = "Press any key to continue"
print(string1) // This will print the above message on the screen
```

- Strings can be manipulated and handled in many ways. Consider the following string:

```
string1 = "Good morning"
print(string1) // This will simply print Good morning
```

```
print(string1.length) // This will return 12, the number of characters
including the space
print(string1.upper) // This will print GOOD MORNING in capitals
print(string1.[6]) // This will print the sixth character: m
print(string1(5, 7) // This will print seven characters, starting from
position 5 (position 0 on the far left), and display: morning
```

- **Concatenation** is the adding together of two strings. For example:

```
string1 = "Good morning"
string2 = "world!"
fullMessage = string1 + string2
print(fullMessage) // This will print Good morning world!
```

File Handling

- Programs often need to access external data in another file. They need to first open the file, then read the file, then write additional data if required and, finally, close the file.
- Consider an external text file called firstNames.txt.
- A file handle called myFile will be a reference to the data:

```
myFile = openRead("firstNames.txt") // This will open the file in read-only mode
lineOne = myFile.readLine() // This will assign the first line as lineOne
lineTwo = myFile.readLine() // This will assign the second line as lineTwo
and so on
myFile.close() // This will close the file
```

> ### Key Point
>
> Reading a file does not edit the contents. Writing will create a new file or overwrite the contents of an existing file

- **Write** mode enables a new file to be created or an existing file to be **overwritten**.
- To replace the list of names in the existing firstNames.txt file:

```
myFile = openWrite("firstNames.txt") // This will open the file in write mode
myFile.writeLine("Isobel") // This will replace the list with a single name
myFile.close() // This will close the file
```

- When reading a file with multiple entries, endOfFile() is used to determine when the end of the file is reached. For example:

```
myFile = openRead("firstNames.txt")
while NOT myFile.endOfFile() // A loop will run until the end of the file is reached
    print(myFile.readLine()) // Each line of the file is now printed
endwhile // The loop will continue until the end of the file is reached
myFile.close() // All entries having been printed, this will close the file
```

> ### Key Words
>
> integer
> Boolean
> real (or float)
> character
> string
> alphanumeric
> casting
> concatenation
> write
> overwritten

 Quick Test

1. Which data type allows decimal places?
2. What term describes two strings added together?
3. Which file-handling mode will replace the contents of a file?

Programming Techniques 2

You must be able to:

- Describe the use of records to store data
- Describe the use of SQL to search data.

Storing Records

- **Databases** are designed for storing large amounts of data, which can be categorized and structured for ease of accessibility.

memberID	userName	age	country	gamerRating
0001	ShonkiD	14	UK	5
0002	Sup3R1	42	USA	7
0003	ch@rlyB	25	UK	4.5

- Data is stored in tables containing **fields** (categories) and **records** (each row of related data).
- The **primary key** is a unique identifiable field that cannot be repeated.
- Imagine a games network user database called Gamers.
- Each field will have a specific data type.
- The primary key is memberID.
- Three records are shown: 0001, 0002 and 0003.
- A **flat-file database** has only one table.
- A **relational database** has multiple databases, linked together by a common key field.

Using Structured Query Language

- **Structured Query Language** (SQL) is a language designed to create, edit and search databases. Consider the games network user database already shown.
  - To create the games network user database with data types:

  > CREATE TABLE Gamers (memberID INTEGER PRIMARY KEY, userName STRING, age INTEGER, country STRING, gamerRating REAL);

  - To search for all usernames in the database:

  > SELECT userName FROM Gamers;

  - To search for a player for whom a condition is met (rating higher than 6):

  > SELECT userName FROM Gamers WHERE gamerRating > 6;

  - To search for a player for whom more than one condition is met (UK and rating less than 6):

  > SELECT userName FROM Gamers WHERE gamerRating < 6 AND country = UK;

  - To search for all users with S as the first letter of their username:

  > SELECT userName FROM Gamers WHERE userName LIKE S&;

  - To order users by their gamer rating in ascending order:

  > SELECT userName FROM Gamers ORDER BY gamerRating ASC;

Quick Test

1. What is a unique field with non-repeatable content called?
2. How many tables does a flat-file database normally contain?
3. Create an SQL search for a field called firstName from a database called addressBook.

Key Words

databases
fields
records
primary key
flat-file database
relational database
Structured Query Language

Programming Techniques 3

You must be able to:

- Use one-dimensional and two-dimensional arrays
- Effectively use sub-programs to help structure code.

Arrays

- An array is a data structure for storing groups within a program, meaning that several pieces of data can be stored under one name or variable.
- A **one-dimensional array** is a single list of common elements.
  - To create an array with seven elements (the days of the week):

```
array week[7]
week[0] = "Sunday"
week[1] = "Monday"
week[2] = "Tueday" // Tuesday has been spelled incorrectly here on purpose
week[3] = "Wednesday"
week[4] = "Thursday"
week[5] = "Friday"
week[6] = "Saturday"
```

  - To print the days of the weekend:

```
print(week[6])
print(week[0])
```

  - To replace an element to correct a spelling:

```
week[2] = "Tuesday" // Completely replacing the element
```

  - Imagine a student with a range of five marks (out of 20) across a school term:

```
score = ["8","12","4","13","20"] // An array can also be created this way
```

  - A 'for' loop could be used to convert all values into a percentage:

```
for i = 0 to 4
    score[i] = score[i] / 20 * 100
next i
```

- In a **two-dimensional array**, each element within the array can have its own array, sometimes called a list of lists. Elements are referenced by their list position within another list. Consider a two-dimensional array of student names and grades.

	0	1	2
0	Liz	9	6
1	Gary	7	9
2	Rebecca	8	10

- To create this array:

```
testScore [3,3] // Declare the rows first and then the columns
testScore = [[Liz, "9","6"],[Gary, "7","9"],[Rebecca, "8","10"]]
```

- To search this array:

```
testScore[2,1] would be 8
```

Sub-programs

- **Sub-programs**, or sub-routines, are used to save time and avoid repetitive code. If a section of code is used multiple times within the same program, it should be saved as a sub-program.
- Sub-programs can contain both **arguments** and **parameters**:
  - Parameters refer to variables within a sub-program.
  - Arguments refer to actual data used by a sub-program.
- Most high-level programming languages have sub-programs built in.
- There are two types of sub-program: **procedures** and **functions**.
- Procedures are a set of instructions that are grouped together and assigned a name. They are called as required by the program to carry out a task, after which the program will continue to run.
  - A procedure for saying thank you when required:

```
procedure thankyou(name)
print("Thank you"+name) // The name variable will be set elsewhere
endprocedure
```

  - A procedure to count from 1 to 10:

```
procedure count()
for x = 1 to 10
next x
endprocedure
```

- Functions are similar to procedures but are designed to return a value that the program will use.
  - A function to generate the first number in a lottery system:

```
function lottery()
    number1 = random(1,49)
return(number1)
endfunction
```

Key Words

one-dimensional array
two-dimensional array
sub-programs
arguments
parameters
procedures
functions

Quick Test

1. Describe two benefits of sub-programs.
2. A list of lists is sometimes used to describe which type of array?
3. Which type of sub-program returns a value?

Producing Robust Programs

You must be able to:

- Describe the term 'defensive design'
- Describe program maintainability
- Understand the importance of testing and using test data
- Describe how to spot program errors.

What is Defensive Design?

- It is important to consider all those who will be using a program and what level of access each user will be given. This can be done in several ways:
  - Use of authentication to check the identity of the user.
  - Use of passwords to prevent unauthorized access.
  - Specific usernames and/or passwords can be given limited functionality.
  - Plan for users making mistakes. Does your program consider the following?
    - o Incorrect login details or forgotten passwords.
    - o Keys pressed and data entered outside your expected ranges.
    - o Users trying to access parts of the program they should not.

Key Point
Design programs to be accessed by users with good intentions and to anticipate users with bad intentions.

Program Maintainability

- A well-maintained program is easy to understand by other programmers; it is also straightforward to access and edit if it needs to be revisited at a later date, which may be required to repair it, improve it or use it as a basis for another program.
- Use the following to keep a program well maintained:

  - **Comments** – personal notes added to lines of code explain an author's thinking and describe functionality (normally using # or // notation).
  - **Indentation** – this separates statements into groups and highlights features.
  - **Variables** – make sure that these are sensibly named and clearly refer to the purpose of the variable.
  - **Sub-routines** – use these sparingly and only when they benefit the program.

Testing and Test Data

- It is essential that a program is tested fully before others are allowed access to it.
- Effective testing checks all functionality and repairs potential errors before external users have access to the program.
- The different types of testing include the ones shown on the next page.

- Iterative testing – a cycle of design, development and testing, in which the results of testing are fed back into the loop to enable redesign and redevelopment as appropriate.
- Final testing is carried out by real users, with the aim of finding issues not considered by the original designer.
- Performance testing – what impact does a program have on system resources?
- Usability testing – is the program user friendly?
- Security testing – is the program vulnerable to attacks and is data secure?
- Load/stress testing – will the program crash if multiple users access it at the same time?

Spotting Program Errors

- Generating errors is a normal part of the program design process. The most common types of error are syntax and logic errors.
  - A **syntax error** is usually spotted by program compilers and interpreters and is specific to the particular programming language in use. In each language there are ways in which certain functions should be formatted. A specific statement may have been typed incorrectly or an incorrect/invalid character may have been used.
  - A **logic error** is a fault in the structure or design of a program. Logic errors are more difficult to spot. Incorrect data types may have been used or lines may simply be in the wrong order, causing the program to crash. Effective and systematic testing is the only way to resolve logic errors.

Test Plans and Test Data

- A **test plan** (or table) outlines all of the elements of a program that can be tested, how to test them, the results and how any errors might be resolved.
- Tests should be listed in a logical order, normally in a table, and cover all functionality, user pathways and potential errors.
- Suitable test data should be created. Test data falls into three categories:

Normal data	Acceptable data likely to be input into the program.
Extreme (or boundary) data	Values at the limit of what a program should be able to handle.
Erroneous (or invalid) data	Values that the program should not accept or process.

- Headings in a test plan may include the following:

Test number	Test description/ reason	Test data to be used	Expected outcome	Actual outcome	Further action if required

 Quick Test

1. Why should individual login details be added to programs that have multiple users?
2. Name two types of error specific to programming languages.

Key Words

iterative testing
syntax error
logic error
test plan
normal data
extreme (or boundary) data
erroneous (or invalid) data

Translators and Facilities of Languages

You must be able to:

- Understand the need for different levels of programming languages
- Describe the purpose of translators
- Describe the characteristics of an assembler, a compiler and an interpreter
- Describe the functionality of an integrated development environment.

The Need for Program Languages

- Computers receive instructions from us through programming languages.
- Binary is the only language that computers understand, so whatever language we use must be translated into binary before it can be processed.

High-Level and Low-Level Languages

- **High-level languages** are written by humans and contain keywords and syntax that programmers understand.
  - Modern high-level languages include:

    o **Python**
    o **Java**
    o **Visual Basic**
    o **C Family** of languages

  - They often share common terminology such as 'if', 'while' and 'until'.
- **Low-level languages** are more difficult to read and write, and they are much closer to direct instructions that a computer can understand. They are often used to directly control hardware.
  - **Machine code** is an example of a low-level language that can execute commands directly without any translation.

> **Key Point**
>
> Machine code can be understood directly by a computer.

Translators

- Any programming language other than machine code must be translated before a computer can understand it.
- Modern **translators** include:
  - **Assemblers** – required to convert low-level languages, such as **assembly language**, into instructions.
  - **Compilers** – used to read high-level languages and convert programs as a whole into machine code programs. Compilers will fail if errors are found, and the process must then begin again.

- **Interpreters** – used to examine a high-level language file one line at a time and convert each instruction into compatible machine code instructions. Although interpreters are slower than compilers, being able to translate while the program is running means that errors within specific lines of code can be identified more quickly.

Integrated Development Environment

- Modern integrated development environment (IDE) software allows programmers to design, develop and test their program ideas.
- Common functionality includes:
  - Code editors – a text editor designed for writing source code. Tools to assist with formatting and syntax and the colour coding of statements help the programmer to spot errors.
  - **Error diagnostics** – also referred to as debugging tools, these will help to identify errors in particular lines of code.
  - **Run-time environment** – this allows programs to be run virtually within the IDE software, testing each line and allowing the programmer to spot and resolve errors.
  - Translators – these will compile or interpret the final code as required.

Key Words

high-level languages
Python
Java
Visual Basic
C Family
low-level languages
machine code
translators
assemblers
assembly language
compilers
interpreters
error diagnostics
run-time environment

Quick Test

1. Which low-level language can a computer understand without translation?
2. Which type of translator converts high-level language one line at a time while the program is running?
3. Name three high-level programming languages.

Where space is not provided, write your answers on a separate piece of paper.

Algorithms and Flow Diagrams

1 Repeating tasks until a certain condition is met is an example of _____ . [1]

2 Match each term with its definition. [3]

Decomposition		The removal of unwanted or unnecessary information from a task.
Abstraction		Being able to identify patterns in data and to build efficient algorithms.
Pattern recognition		Breaking tasks into smaller tasks that are easier to understand.

3 The number 14 in the following list cannot be searched for using a binary search. Why not? [1]

1 3 6 7 9 14 12

_____

4 Describe briefly how a merge sort works. [3]

_____

_____

_____

5 What is the purpose of the lines and arrows in an algorithm flow diagram? [1]

_____

6 Calling on a predefined sequence at different points of a flow diagram would be an example

of using a _____ . [1]

7 Printing an on-screen message would normally be represented by which symbol? [1]

_____

Pseudocode 1

1 Which common pseudocode keyword is used to create loops? **[1]**

2 Using a capital letter instead of a space to show a second word is an example of

_____. **[1]**

3 What is the value named conversionFactor in the following code an example of? **[1]**

_____.

```
costInPounds = costInPence / conversionFactor
```

4 What value should conversionFactor in the previous question be assigned? **[1]**

5 What part of the code below is a comment? **[1]**

```
print("Thank you and goodbye") // This closes the program
```

6 What does the following code do? **[3]**

```
quizAnswer = ""
while quizChoice == ""
    letter = input("Please select an answer, either A, B or C.")
    if quizChoice == "" then
        print("You haven't made a choice yet.")
    endif
endwhile
```

Pseudocode 2

1 Fill in the missing word in the following sentence.

_____ operators are sometimes referred to as relational operators. **[1]**

2 Match each term with its definition. **[3]**

Boolean operators	Used to test the relationship between two values.
Arithmetic operators	Used to define relationships using logical operators.
Comparison operators	Used in mathematical calculations in pseudocode.

3 Explain the difference between a single equals sign = and a double equals sign == with respect to operators. **[2]**

4 What operators are required to represent the following functions?

   a) Less than. _____ **[1]**

   b) Greater than. _____ **[1]**

   c) Less than or equal to. _____ **[1]**

   d) Greater than or equal to. _____ **[1]**

5 Which arithmetic operator returns the remainder after a division? **[1]**

6 Which Boolean operator can be used to return a true response if either of two statements is true? **[1]**

7 When swapping between pseudocode and programming languages such as Python or JavaScript, why should care be taken when writing code? **[1]**

Computational Logic

1 Which logic gate is represented by a triangle? [1]

....

2 Complete the following AND gate truth table. [4]

Inputs		Output
A	B	Q
0	0	
1	0	
0	1	
1	1	

3 What do B, C and X represent in the following diagram? [2]

....

....

4 If an AND gate and a NOT gate are connected in series, what would be the output of the NOT gate if both inputs to the AND gate were turned off? [1]

....

5 If a binary logic diagram has four inputs, how many possible outputs are there? [1]

....

6 Which gate will give a true output if one or more of its inputs is high? [1]

....

7 Fill in the missing word in the following sentence.

In a truth table, 0s and 1s are used to represent .... [2]

Where space is not provided, write your answers on a separate piece of paper.

Programming Techniques 1

1 Match each term with its definition. [5]

Integer	A single letter, number or symbol.
Boolean	A whole number with no decimal point.
Real (or float)	A collection of alphanumeric data characters and symbols.
Character	Digital data – can present only two values.
String	All numbers, including those with a decimal point.

2 The following would be examples of which data type: 4.32, 0.3, –4.5? [1]

3 Define the term 'casting'. [1]

4 What would be the purpose of the following code? [1]

```
str(42)
```

5 Strings are normally contained within which symbols? [1]

6 What is the following code an example of? [1]

```
string1 = "Good Evening"
string2 = "Everyone."
fullMessage = string1 + string2
print(fullMessage)
```

7 Describe the difference between the two file-handling terms 'openRead' and 'openWrite'. [2]

8 Which code would normally be used to determine when the end of a multiple entry file is reached? [1]

9 What would be the function of the following code?   [3]

```
myFile = openWrite("petNames.txt")
myFile.writeLine("Poppy")
myFile.close()
```

Programming Techniques 2

1 Complete the following paragraph using the words from the box.

fields	primary key	Data	records	tables

_____ is stored in _____ containing _____

(categories) and _____ (each row of related data). The _____

is a unique identifiable field that cannot be repeated.   [5]

2 Describe the difference between a flat-file database and a relational database.   [2]

3 What does the abbreviation SQL stand for?   [1]

4 Briefly describe the purpose of the following SQL command.   [3]

```
SELECT surnameName FROM Classlist WHERE examScore > 80
```

5 Write a similar SQL command to search for the first name of a student with an examination score of 55.   [3]

Programming Techniques 3

1 Define the term 'array'.   [2]

2 The phrase 'list of lists' is often used to describe what type of array?   [1]

3 Variables within a sub-program (or sub-routine) are referred to as _____.   [1]

4 Name the **two** types of sub-program.   [2]

Producing Robust Programs

1 Describe **four** methods of defensive design that a programmer would use when considering user access. **[4]**

2 Why is it important to ensure that a program is well maintained? **[2]**

3 In addition to using comments, list **three** more maintenance tips. **[3]**

4 Describe the difference between performance testing and load/stress testing. **[2]**

5 Incorrectly typed functions and character-based mistakes in coding are usually described as which type of error? **[1]**

6 Match each term with its definition. **[3]**

Normal data	Values the program should not accept or process.
Extreme data	Acceptable data likely to be input into the program.
Erroneous data	Values at the limit of what a program can handle.

7 Describe the need for a test plan when designing a program for commercial purposes. **[2]**

8 Give **five** headings that may form part of a test table. **[5]**

Translators and Facilities of Languages

1 What is the difference between high-level programming languages and low-level programming languages? **[2]**

2 The only true language that a computer can understand is _____. **[1]**

3 Give an example of a low-level programming language. **[1]**

4 Describe the purpose of a programming translator. **[2]**

5 Match each translator type with its description. **[3]**

Assemblers	Used to read high-level languages and convert programs as a whole into machine code programs.
Compilers	Examine high-level language files one line at a time and convert each instruction into compatible machine code instructions.
Interpreters	Required to convert low-level languages, such as assembly language, into instructions.

6 Which type of translator will analyse, run and convert a high-level language file one line at a time? **[1]**

7 What does the abbreviation IDE stand for? **[1]**

8 List **four** functions of a modern IDE. **[4]**

9 Colour coding scripts and highlighting syntax errors are features of which IDE function? **[1]**

Units and Formats of Data

You must be able to:

- Explain why a computer can process data only in a binary format
- Describe common units of data
- Describe how binary codes are used to represent characters
- Explain the term 'character set'
- Describe the relationship between character bits and sets.

Binary and Units of Data

- Computers communicate and process instructions using binary. Each single character or set of instructions must be converted into a series of 0s and 1s that represent electrical flow (0 = off, 1 = on).
- As we do not speak binary and computers cannot be programmed without it, all instructions must be translated.
- Common units of data are shown in the table below:

> **Key Point**
>
> One numerical character = 1 byte.

Name	Size	Typical examples
Bit (b)	1 binary digit	0 or 1.
Nibble	4 bits	Half an 8-bit sequence, used in hexadecimal.
Byte (B)	8 bits	Large enough to store one character (F, for example).
Kilobyte (KB)	1000 bytes	Small documents and text files.
Megabyte (MB)	1000 kilobytes	Computer documents, music files and images.
Gigabyte (GB)	1000 megabytes	High-resolution videos and games.
Terabyte (TB)	1000 gigabytes	Capacity of large backup storage drives.
Petabyte (PB)	1000 terabytes	International cloud storage systems.

Please note you may also see sizes referred to as 1024 rather than 1000. This is because 1024 is a power of 2 in relation to binary calculations.

010011010
001101001
00011001
0101110
0010001

Character Sets

- Communicating and programming in binary is extremely difficult and time-consuming.
- **Character sets** were created to bridge the gap, allowing alphanumeric characters that we recognize to be typed into a computer and converted into a usable binary equivalent.
- Common character sets include:
  - **ASCII** (American Standard Code for Information Interchange), which was created to allow computer manufacturers in the English-speaking world to share a common coding standard. Originally a 7-bit code with 128 possible characters, an extra zero (bit) was added to every binary sequence to create an 8-bit (1-byte) character set.

Key Point

Take a look at the full ASCII table online (for example at www.ascii-code.com).

ASCII coding groups

ASCII Number	8-Bit Binary	Character
120	01111000	x
121	01111001	y
122	01111010	z
123	01111011	{
124	01111100	|
125	01111101	}
126	01111110	~

Sample from ASCII table

ASCII Range	Value or Function
0–32	Unprintable control codes
33–47	Symbols and punctuation
48–57	Digital 0–9
58–64	More symbols
65–90	Upper-case letters A–Z
91–96	More symbols
97–122	Lower-case letters a–z
123–127	More symbols

- **Extended ASCII**, which extended the sequence to a full 8-bit system allowing 256 characters. This extends its use to European languages that require accents or extra symbols.
- **Unicode**, which was developed as a world industry standard to represent all known languages using 16-bit and 32-bit binary codes.

Key Point

Unicode was developed to set worldwide common coding standards.

Key Words

character sets
ASCII
extended ASCII
unicode

Quick Test

1. How many bits are there in a nibble?
2. Why was an extra zero added to the original ASCII code?
3. How many characters can extended ASCII represent?

Converting Data 1

You must be able to:

- Convert denary numbers into binary numbers
- Perform simple binary calculations
- Explain the terms 'binary overflow' and 'binary shift'.

Converting Denary into Binary

Key Point

Denary is another word for decimal.

- **Denary**, or decimal, is our standard number system. It is a **base 10** system with 10 digits (0, 1, 2, 3, 4, 5, 6, 7, 8, 9).
- **Binary** is a base 2 number system and is the language of computers. The first eight numbers of base 2 look like this:

128	64	32	16	8	4	2	1

- An 8-bit structure replaces each number with a binary switch (1 or 0, on or off).
- The sequence 00000001 would generate a total of 1.
- The sequence 11111111 would generate a total of 255.
- Using each binary switch, we can represent the denary numbers 0–255 (256 characters) as binary numbers and vice versa:
    - Converting denary into binary:
      198 = 11000110 (128 + 64 + 0 + 0 + 0 + 4 + 2 + 0).
    - Converting binary into denary:
      01010001 = 81 (0 + 64 + 0 + 16 + 0 + 0 + 0 + 1).

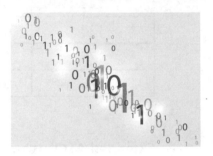

Binary Calculations

- Binary numbers can be added together. For example, to work out the following:
    - 01010011 + 01110110
    - Work from the right and use these four rules, carrying under to the left as required:

Rule One:	0 + 0 = 0
Rule Two:	1 + 0 = 1
Rule Three:	1 + 1 = 10 (binary for 2)
Rule Four:	1 + 1 + 1 = 11 (binary for 3)

```
  01010011          83
+ 01110110        +118
  11001001         201
  1 1 1   1 1
```

Binary Overflow

- 8-bit binary has a maximum value of 11111111 (255).
- Anything over this value, for example 278, will produce an **overflow error**.
- This is because all 8 bits have been used and there is nowhere for the additional digit to be stored or handled.

Binary Shift

- When working directly with binary numbers, a **binary shift** to the left and right can be used for multiplication and division, respectively.
  - A **left shift** will multiply a binary number by 2^N (where N is the number of shifts to the left).

  For example, a left shift of 1 (binary number × 2^1):

  0 0 1 0 1 1 0 0 (44)

  0 1 0 1 1 0 0 0 (88)

  - A **right shift** will divide a binary number by 2^N (where N is the number of shifts to the right).

  For example, a right shift of 1 (binary number ÷ 2^1):

  0 0 1 0 0 1 1 0 (38)

  0 0 0 1 0 0 1 1 (19)

An example of binary code

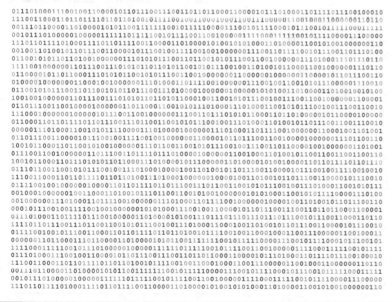

Quick Test

1. Convert 196 into binary.
2. What is an overflow error?
3. Multiplying a binary number by four will require a left shift of . . .?

Key Words

denary
base 10
binary
overflow error
binary shift

Converting Data 2

You must be able to:

- Convert binary numbers into hexadecimal numbers
- Convert hexadecimal numbers into denary numbers.

Hexadecimal

- **Hexadecimal** is a convenient way for programmers to express large binary numbers.
- Computers do not understand hexadecimal; it is simply a shortcut reference for programmers.
- It is a **base 16** number system and uses digits and letters.
  - Remember binary is base 2 (two digits: 0, 1).
  - Denary is base 10 (10 digits: 0, 1, 2, 3, 4, 5, 6, 7, 8, 9).
  - Hexadecimal is base 16 (16 digits and letters: 0, 1, 2, 3, 4, 5, 6, 7, 8, 9, A, B, C, D, E, F).
  - The use of letters prevents the duplication of numbers.

NUMERAL SYSTEMS

Decimal (base 10)	Binary (base 2)	Hexadecimal (base 16)	Decimal (base 10)	Binary (base 2)	Hexadecimal (base 16)
0	0000	0	8	1000	8
1	0001	1	9	1001	9
2	0010	2	10	1010	A
3	0011	3	11	1011	B
4	0100	4	12	1100	C
5	0101	5	13	1101	D
6	0110	6	14	1110	E
7	0111	7	15	1111	F

Converting Binary into Hexadecimal

- One hexadecimal digit can be used to represent a **nibble** (4 bits), meaning that two digits can represent one byte (8 bits).
- For example:

0	1	1	0	1	0	1	1

Divided into two nibbles:

0	1	1	0		1	0	1	1

Converted into separate denary numbers:

6   **11**

Represented in hexadecimal:

6B

Base 2 binary	Base 10 denary	Base 16 hexadecimal
0000	0	0
0001	1	1
0010	2	2
0011	3	3
0100	4	4
0101	5	5
0110	6	6
0111	7	7
1000	8	8
1001	9	9
1010	10	A
1011	11	B
1100	12	C
1101	13	D
1110	14	E
1111	15	F

Converting Hexadecimal into Denary

- Converting hexadecimal into denary involves converting each digit into its denary equivalent, multiplying by its base 16 position using the table below and adding the values together.

16^3	16^2	16^1	16^0
4096	256	16	1

- Using the example of 6F:
  - Convert each digit into its denary equivalent:
  - (6 is represented by 6) and (F is represented by 15)
  - $6F = (6 \times 16^1) + (15 \times 16^0)$
  - $6F = (96) + (15)$
  - $6F = 111$.

Check Digit

- A **check digit** system is used when a program input needs a certain range of numbers to run correctly.
- An algorithm is run to check the data entered and an error response is given if the data does not fall within the specified criteria.
- The check digit is normally the last one on the right and is calculated using an algorithm applied to the other digits in the sequence.
- Examples include:
  - the ISBN (International Standard Book Number) system used to number and catalogue books
  - a particular number within a passport number
  - the last digit of a bank card number.

Quick Test

1. Convert 00110101 into hexadecimal.
2. Convert 13A into denary.
3. Which part of a number does a check digit normally look at first?

Key Words

hexadecimal
base 16
nibble
check digit

Audio/Visual Formats and Compression

You must be able to:

- Describe how images can be represented in binary
- Explain the terms 'metadata', 'colour depth' and 'resolution'
- Describe how sound can be stored digitally
- Explain the terms 'sampling', 'bit rate' and 'sampling frequency'
- Describe audio/visual compression techniques.

Images and Binary

- Images saved electronically are made up of a series of pixels – tiny dots in neat lines. Changing the colour or brightness of each pixel is what generates detail.
- All computer data is binary, and an image can be converted into binary by using a binary code to represent each pixel.

> The example below uses only two colours, each represented using 0 or 1.
> - 1-bit image: two colours (1^2), 0 or 1.
> - 2-bit image: four colours (2^2), 00, 01, 10 and 11.
> - More colours can be added using longer binary codes.

0	1	1	1	1	0
1	1	1	1	1	1
1	0	1	1	0	1
1	1	1	1	1	1
0	1	0	0	1	0
1	0	1	1	0	1

- **Colour depth** is the number of bits per pixel. A 4-bit image has 16 colours (2^4). Most modern devices use a 24-bit colour depth (2^{24}), with 16,777,216 colours.
- The more pixels used to create an image, the more detail displayed and the higher the **resolution**.
- An image file size is determined by its size in pixels and by the colour depth.

> For example, consider a 24-bit image of 800 × 600 pixels:
> - 800 × 600 = 480,000 pixels
> - 480,000 × 24 bits = 11,520,000 bits
> - 11,520,000 ÷ 8 (8 bits in 1 byte) = 1,440,000 bytes or 1.44 megabytes.

- **Metadata**. In addition to the image itself, information can be stored within the same image file. This information can include but is not limited to:
  - Technical data generated by the camera – aperture and shutter speed, resolution, **GPS location**, date and time.
  - Data added manually by the user – place names or captions, comments or people's names, the name of the photographer's business or copyright information.

> **Key Point**
>
> Modern cameras and smartphones add GPS location data as metadata.

Sound

- Live sound, recorded by a microphone, is called **analogue** sound.
- Live analogue sound is continuously changing and has many complex variables.
- To store sound on a computer, it must be converted into a digital file with a mathematical structure. This is called **sampling**.
- Sampling records and measures the sound at regular time intervals. The number of samples taken each second is the **sampling frequency**.
- The higher the sample rate, the better quality the sound file. Compact discs have a sample rate of 44,100 or 44.1 kHz (kilohertz).
- The **bit rate** is the number of bits used to encode the sample. Compact discs use a bit rate of 16.

> For example, consider a 4-minute stereo music track with a standard sample rate:
>
> - 240 × 44,100 × 16 = 169,344,000 bits
> - 169,344,000 × 2 (stereo tracks) = 338,688,000 bits
> - 338,688,000 bits ÷ 8 (8 bits in 1 byte) = 42,336,000 bytes or 42,336 MB.

Compression

- Modern high-quality graphic and audio files have large file sizes. As we constantly create new files, and storage space on devices is limited, **data compression** can be used to reduce large file sizes. There are several benefits of data compression:
  - Storage space required on mobile devices and home computers can be reduced.
  - Smaller files can be uploaded and downloaded more quickly.
  - Limits placed on file sizes by streaming and email services can be avoided.
- The balance between quality and file size, especially with audio and visual data, has led to the creation of different compression methods:
  - **Lossy compression** removes data, for example duplicated elements, to create a smaller file size. Any data removed during the compression is removed permanently.
    - o Popular lossy file types include JPEG, MP3, GIF and MP4.
  - **Lossless compression** uses software algorithms to compress data but then reconstructs it into its original form, preserving the original file.
    - o Popular lossless file types include RAW, WAV, TIFF and BMP.

Quick Test

1. An image file is made up of 17,488,000 bits. How many megabytes is this?
2. Name a popular music file format that uses a high level of compression.
3. A music producer is creating master copies of a new track. Which compression method should they use and why?

Key Words

colour depth
resolution
metadata
GPS location
analogue
sampling
sampling frequency
bit rate
data compression
lossy compression
lossless compression

Where space is **not** provided, write your answers on a separate piece of paper.

Programming Techniques 1

1 Give the pseudocode version of each of the following data types.

a) Integer .... [1]

b) Boolean .... [1]

c) Real .... [1]

d) Character .... [1]

e) String .... [1]

2 $, &, T and e are examples of which data type? [1]

....

3 The process of converting a string into an integer or converting a number into a string

is called .... [1]

4 Write a short program that defines the phrase "Good morning Dave" as string 1
and then prints the string. [2]

5 Adding two strings together to create a single string is called .... [1]

6 Consider the following string.

```
string1 = "Hello world!"
```

What would the following three lines of code print?

a)
```
print(string1.length)
```

b)
```
print(string1.upper)
```

c)
```
print(string1.[3])
```
[3]

7 What must always be considered when using the openWrite function with an existing file? **[1]**

Programming Techniques 2

1 In a database with the following fields, which field should be used as a primary key and why? **[2]**

identNumber	firstName	surname	postCode

2 To create a relational database, what must each table have? **[1]**

3 Briefly describe the purpose of SQL. **[2]**

4 Within a SQL database, what is the purpose of the term ASC? **[1]**

Programming Techniques 3

1 Using code, create an array of the four seasons. **[2]**

2 Alternatively, an array can be defined in one line. Write an example line of code to specify a range of four different temperatures in the 20s. **[3]**

3 Based on the following table, called carSurvey, write a two-line piece of code that would create a two-dimensional array. **[4]**

Cars	6	9
Bikes	4	3
Vans	6	6

4 What would the following search return? **[1]**

```
carSurvey[0,2]
```

5 Describe a key difference between a sub-program procedure and a sub-program function. **[2]**

Producing Robust Programs

1 Creating access-limited usernames and passwords and planning for user error are examples of .... [1]

2 Using sub-routines and using user-friendly comments in coding are examples of

.... [1]

3 Who should a programmer plan for? Tick the correct answer. [1]

   A Experienced computer users. ☐

   B Users who will make mistakes. ☐

   C Users who try to break the program. ☐

   D All of the above. ☐

4 Which of the following would be a poorly named variable and why? Tick the correct box and answer on the line underneath. [2]

   A lastName ☐   **B** emailAddress ☐   **C** dataStuff ☐

5 In addition to performance testing, name **five** types of program testing. [5]

6 An incorrectly spelt function or a misplaced character will normally return which type of error when a program is run? [1]

7 Consider a program that asks for the month of the year in numerical format. Provide examples for the following test data categories.

   a) Normal data. [1]

   b) Extreme data. [1]

   c) Erroneous data. [1]

8 What is the difference between an expected outcome and the actual outcome in a standard test table? **[2]**

Translators and Facilities of Languages

1 Why are low-level languages more difficult to read and write than high-level languages? **[1]**

2 Briefly describe the purpose of a compiler. **[1]**

3 Why must a compiler restart any conversion if an error is found? **[1]**

4 Which type of translator is designed to work with low-level languages? **[1]**

5 When programming manufacturing equipment, what would be a major benefit of using an IDE? **[2]**

6 Which function of an IDE allows for virtual program testing? **[1]**

Where space is not provided, write your answers on a separate piece of paper.

Units and Formats of Data

1 A modern office considering a backup system would most likely need it to have a capacity in the order of which size? Tick the correct answer.

   A Kilobytes. ☐

   B Terabytes. ☐

   C Nibbles. ☐ [1]

2 How many bits would be required to save the word 'data'? [1]

3 How many gigabytes is 6144 MB equal to? [1]

4 Briefly describe the term 'character set'. [2]

5 What is the abbreviation ASCII short for? [1]

6 How many characters did the original ASCII set represent? [1]

7 Why was an extra zero added to the original ASCII binary equivalent? [2]

8 Name the character set designed to represent all known languages. [1]

Converting Data 1

1 State the number base system of the following.

    a) Denary .... **[1]**

    b) Binary .... **[1]**

2 Convert the following binary numbers into denary.

    a) 00000001 .... **[1]**

    b) 11111111 .... **[1]**

    c) 10110101 .... **[1]**

    d) 00110011 .... **[1]**

    e) 01010101 .... **[1]**

    f) 11110000 .... **[1]**

3 Add the following binary numbers: 10110101 and 00110011. **[1]**

....

4 What is the highest possible 8-bit binary value and why? **[2]**

....

....

5 Briefly describe the term 'binary overflow'. **[1]**

....

6 What would be the effect on a binary number of:

    a) a left shift of 1? **[1]**

....

    b) a right shift of 1? **[1]**

....

Converting Data 2

1 List the 16 digits in the base 16 number system. [1]

2 The primary purpose of hexadecimal for programmers is to _____. [1]

3 Why are letters used in the hexadecimal system? [1]

4 Convert the following binary numbers into hexadecimal.

a) 00110001 [1]

b) 10101101 [1]

c) 01111110 [1]

d) 11100001 [1]

5 Convert the following hexadecimal numbers into denary.

a) 6D [1]

b) 3B [1]

c) 75 [1]

6 A _____ system is run to check the data entered, and an error response is given if the data does not fall within the specified criteria. [1]

Audio/Visual Formats and Compression

1 Match each term with its definition. **[3]**

Metadata	The number of bits per pixel.
Colour depth	The number of pixels used to create an image.
Resolution	Additional information saved within the image file.

2 List in binary the **four** colours of a 2-bit image. **[4]**

3 How many pixels would form a mobile phone screen with a resolution of 1334 × 750? **[1]**

4 Compact discs are usually created with a bit rate of .... **[1]**

5 Calculate the file size of a mono audio track of 3 minutes with a standard sample rate of 44,100 and a bit rate of 16. **[1]**

6 Explain why recording at a higher sample rate will create a larger digital audio file. **[1]**

7 Describe a potential danger of using image compression. **[1]**

8 List **three** popular compressed file types used to store sound or images. **[3]**

9 *Lossy compression can never be returned to its original state once saved.* True or false? **[1]**

To complete the programming project, you must be able to:
* Understand the main requirements of the non-examination project
* Describe the key programming skills required
* Carry out a detailed analysis of the project requirements.

Non-Examination Assessment

Following one of the examination board set assignments, you will create a coded solution within the 20-hour time limit.

The key elements are:

* project analysis and success criteria (what a successful solution will be able to do)
* planning and design (flow charts and pseudocode)
* development (narrative of the process with explanations of code)
* testing and remedial actions (with explanations of changes made)
* evaluation (clearly linked to success criteria).

You can use any of the following high-level programming languages:

* Python
* C Family of languages (for example C#, C++)
* Java
* JavaScript
* Visual Basic/.Net
* PHP
* Delphi
* SQL
* BASH.

Make sure to choose a high-level programming language from the list.

Programming Techniques

The following skills, covered on pages 62–107, are expected to be demonstrated in your project:

* the use of variables, operators, inputs, outputs and assignments
* sequence, selection and iteration programming constructs
* the use of count and condition controlled loops
* multiple data types: Boolean, string, integer and real
* basic string manipulation
* file handling operations: open, read, write and close
* defining arrays
* the use of functions and sub-programs to create well-structured code.

Project Analysis

To design a practical solution, the brief must be broken down in a logical, structured way using computational thinking:

- **Decomposition** – breaking tasks into smaller, manageable problems.
- **Abstraction** – the removal of unwanted data.
- **Pattern recognition** – identifying patterns in data and taking advantage of them.

Consider the following questions:

- What are the key requirements of the brief?
- How can this be broken down into tasks and sub-tasks that will form a detailed **specification**?
- What numerical or alphanumeric data will form part of the solution and what forms will it take?
- What data processing will need to take place with regard to input, output and validation?
- What **success criteria** will allow the solution to be judged against the original brief?
- What tests could be carried out to ensure the following:
  - Have all of the key requirements been met?
  - Does the solution meet the specification?
  - How user friendly is the program?
  - What happens if extreme, incorrect or out-of-range data is entered?

> A detailed specification is essential for effective testing and the refinement of code.

Key Words

specification
success criteria

You must be able to:

- Design algorithms to meet the needs of a brief
- Combine the input, output and processing of appropriate data
- Create a solution that uses sub-routines and appropriate validation
- Develop a clearly explained working coded solution
- Fully test the solution against the needs of the brief
- Critically evaluate the solution and present your findings.

Designing a Solution

Based on the analysis of the brief, a clearly documented system should be designed that includes:

- mind maps of ideas
- flow charts or diagrams
- variables, input and output formats
- data types
- well-structured pseudocode with:
  - functions
  - sub-routines
  - comments explaining functionality and processing
- user navigation and consideration of potential misuse
- potential coding techniques and strategies to be used in later development
- consideration of suitable tests to be carried out during development.

Development

Working from your designs, the development of a solution should be clearly documented and include the following:

- a clear commentary of decisions made throughout the project
- a logical approach to problems that arose and how they were resolved
- evidence of the coding techniques and strategies used
- evidence of progression through the ongoing testing and refinement of code
- accurately recorded sources of data and externally sourced coding libraries
- the creation of any GUI
- code written in a suitable high-level language that includes:
  - comments within your code explaining functionality
  - the use of sub-routines
  - well-named variables
  - a logical, modular structure that can be easily understood
  - the efficient use of functions – excess lines of code are a distraction.

Testing

A detailed test plan will consider all aspects of the initial project brief and your subsequent analysis, including:

- the key features of the initial brief
- the specification written during your analysis
- user functionality and any GUI
- test input data, including extreme and unexpected data
- testing to destruction with the intention of generating a program crash.

The results of all tests should be clearly discussed, including how failed tests could be resolved with more time.

Evaluation and Conclusions

A final report should be produced, covering all aspects of the project from initial ideas to final testing.

It should be logically structured using technical vocabulary, without spelling or grammatical mistakes, and should include the following elements:

- a comparison of the finished project with the initial brief
- a summary of the tests carried out
- the strengths and weaknesses of your solution
- any appropriate user feedback
- potential improvements given more time
- issues encountered and resolved throughout the project
- concluding comments based on evidence.

Where space is not provided, write your answers on a separate piece of paper.

Units and Formats of Data

1 Suggest a suitable size for a memory card holding 300 MP3 files (around 3 MB each). **[1]**

2 Half an 8-bit sequence is called what? Tick the correct answer.

A Byte ☐

B Binary digit ☐

C Nibble ☐ **[1]**

3 *The ASCII character set was originally designed for English characters only.* True or false? **[1]**

4 Complete the following paragraph using the words in the box. **[4]**

European	Extended	accents	256

_____ ASCII extends the sequence to a full 8-bit system allowing

_____ characters. This extends its use to _____ languages

requiring _____ and extra symbols.

5 Briefly describe the purpose of Unicode. **[2]**

6 Fill in the missing word in the following sentence.

Unprintable control codes and upper-case letters A–Z are examples of _____. **[1]**

Converting Data 1

1 Denary and .... are interchangeable terms. [1]

2 List the first eight place values in base 2. [1]

....

3 Convert the following denary numbers into binary using 8-bit only.

a) 60. .... [1]

b) 189. .... [1]

c) 40. .... [1]

d) 11. .... [1]

e) 257. .... [1]

f) 99. .... [1]

4 How many shifts to the left would be required to multiply a binary number by 4? [1]

....

5 Carry out a right shift of 3 on the binary number 01010000. Show the denary equivalent before and after the shift. [3]

....

....

....

6 Why is the highest value in 8-bit binary 255 and not 256? [1]

....

Converting Data 2

1 Hexadecimal is a base .... number system. **[1]**

2 How many hexadecimal digits are used to represent 1 byte? **[1]**

3 Convert the following hexadecimal numbers into binary.

    a) 8B. .... **[1]**

    b) 11. .... **[1]**

    c) 3F. .... **[1]**

    d) F2. .... **[1]**

4 Give **three** examples of when a check digit system might be used to detect errors in data. **[3]**

5 *A computer can read hexadecimal without translation.* True or false? **[1]**

6 Convert the following denary numbers into hexadecimal.

    a) 199. **[1]**

    b) 50. **[1]**

    c) 242. **[1]**

Audio/Visual Formats and Compression

1. Images are made up of tiny dots known as _____. [1]

2. Using two-colour binary (0 = white, 1 = black), create a binary sequence to represent the image shown. [2]

3. List **three** pieces of information that can be found in image metadata. [3]

4. How many colours does an 8-bit image contain? [1]

5. Calculate the file size of an 8-bit image with a resolution of 800 × 600 pixels. [3]

6. Name the process of converting analogue sound into a digital format. [1]

7. Briefly describe the term 'audio sample rate'. [1]

8. Describe **three** benefits of audio/visual data compression. [3]

9. Why might lossless compression be popular with film editors? [2]

Mixed Questions

1　Convert the hexadecimal number 3E into a decimal number. [2]

2　Identify **three** common secondary storage technologies. [3]

3　Richard decides to use an IDE (Integrated Development Environment) to create a new game.

Identify **two** features of the IDE that Richard might use. [2]

4　Add together the following 8-bit binary numbers and show your answer in 8-bit and denary form. [3]

00101010

01000111

5　Why might the touch screen of a smartphone be described as an input and an output device? [2]

6 Describe the fetch–decode–execute cycle as a sequence of **four** events. [4]

7 A newspaper office's computer has been attacked by a virus, and the newspaper's owners have been told that the virus is a form of ransomware.

What does the term 'ransomware' mean? [2]

8 Many people still use the terms 'World Wide Web' and 'the Internet' to mean the same thing.

Explain the difference between these terms. [2]

9 Write a short program using pseudocode that asks the user for their first and last name, and then uses concatenation to print both names on screen as the user's full name. [3]

Mixed Questions

10 Credit and debit cards contain a check digit to ensure that card numbers are read and processed correctly.

Explain the idea behind a check digit.   [2]

_____

_____

11 Helen has written a puzzle game using a high-level programming language. She can use either a compiler or an interpreter to translate the code.

Describe the differences between these methods.   [2]

_____

_____

12 An estate agent is setting up a new office with a new network.

Describe **three** ways in which the information stored on computers can be kept secure.   [3]

_____

_____

_____

13 Convert the decimal number 191 into an 8-bit binary number.   [1]

_____

14 Which network protocol would an online email server use?   [1]

_____

15 A social network web page has a feature that allows users to upload a photo. To prevent the server from being filled too quickly, a 1-MB limit needs to be applied.

Write a pseudocode sub-routine that would do this. [6]

16 In relation to a CPU and motherboard, explain the term 'bus'. [2]

17 A lead designer in a programming team wants to make sure that the code they write can be easily followed by their team members at a later date.

Describe **four** ways of achieving this. [4]

18 Place the following units in order, from largest to smallest. [1]

GB　　**bit**　　**PB**　　**byte**　　**nibble**　　**MB**

Mixed Questions

19 A young family is setting up the wireless network in their new home. They have options for **three** different encryption standards.

Name them, and explain which one the family should use and why. **[3]**

_____

_____

_____

20 Rachel is buying secondary storage to back up her family photos.

State **four** characteristics of secondary storage she should consider when shopping. **[4]**

_____

_____

_____

_____

21 Explain the difference between a database field and a record. **[2]**

_____

_____

22 A desktop computer is running at full capacity and needs to create 'virtual memory' to try to help the machine to run more smoothly.

Explain the term 'virtual memory'. **[2]**

_____

_____

23 A new RPG game is being designed by a small team of programmers.

Explain how defensive design considerations will help them to maintain the game once it has been launched. [4]

....

....

....

....

24 The owners of a large clothing store have chosen a star topology for their LAN.

Provide **four** possible reasons that they have done this. [4]

....

....

....

....

25 Carry out a merge sort on the following numbers. [2]

57, 32, 4, 5, 40, 54, 2

....

....

26 Daniel's new coffee maker contains an embedded system.

What is meant by the term 'embedded system'? [2]

....

....

Mixed Questions

27 Explain the difference between a single equals sign and a double equals sign when writing code. [2]

....

....

....

28 A school is considering moving the storage of student document folders to a cloud-based system.

Describe **two** advantages of doing this. [4]

....

....

....

....

....

29 As programmers started to collaborate all around the world, explain why the Unicode character set had to be created. [2]

....

....

....

30 A musical keyboard program uses sub-routines for each musical note.

Explain **two** benefits of using sub-routines. [2]

....

....

....

31 *Decimal, base 10 and denary are all counting systems based on the digits 0 and 1.*

True or false? .... [1]

32 Lee has been told to look for the HTTPS symbol when shopping online for a new mountain bike.

Why is this a good idea? [2]

....

....

33 A library customer database has the following fields.

memberID	surname	firstName	houseNo	postCode

a) Identify a suitable field to use as a primary key. [1]

....

b) Why does the database need a primary key? [1]

....

34 Explain the difference between volatile and non-volatile memory, and provide an example of each. [4]

....

....

....

....

35 Carry out a bubble sort on the following numbers. [2]

14, 22, 12, 18

....

....

36 A software programmer is starting to design a new work processor. He has been given a large list of requirements and design features to include.

Explain how abstraction will help the designer make a start. **[2]**

_____

_____

37 Describe **three** modern household devices that may contain an embedded system. **[3]**

_____

_____

_____

38 Annie, a university student, has been introduced to a new peer-to-peer network by a friend.

What concerns might she have about using it? **[3]**

_____

_____

_____

39 A bank account program requires users to enter their date of birth in the format DD/MM/YYYY.

State examples of normal, extreme and erroneous data. **[3]**

_____

_____

_____

40 _Open source software is usually purchased through a licence, and the software cannot be edited or shared in any way._

True or false? _____ **[1]**

41 Keeping up with the latest gadgets and smartphones means that our devices are replaced regularly and are designed with a short life span.

What impact does this have on the environment? [4]

....

....

....

....

42 A community centre is delivering a talk to members on the dangers of social engineering.

Describe **three** methods the members should be made aware of. [3]

....

....

....

....

43 A graphic designer's computer is slowing down, and her friend has recommended defragmenting the hard drive.

Describe why this might help. [3]

....

....

....

....

44 A politician with controversial views has had his website closed by a denial of service attack.

Explain this method of network threat. [2]

....

....

....

Answers

Pages 6–7
1. The ALU
2. This refers to a physical pathway shared by signals to and from components of a computer system
3. Any four of the following: keyboard; microphone; mouse; webcam; sensor; drawing tablet; scanner

Pages 8–9
1. GHz
2. Each core is an individual CPU; tasks can be carried out simultaneously
3. a) Printer – embedded paper feed system
   b) Laptop – embedded webcam system
   c) Backup server – embedded temperature control system

Pages 10–11
1. RAM
2. Usually because the installed RAM is full
3. a) No moving parts
   b) Faster data access
   c) Lightweight

Pages 12–13
1. a) They are cheap to manufacture and reproduce
   b) The size and shape is child friendly to handle and load
   c) They are easy to package and are portable
2. It has complex moving parts that will fail if the device is knocked or dropped
3. a) Smartphones
   b) Lightweight laptops
   c) Digital cameras
   d) USB storage devices
   e) Portable media players

The Purpose and Function of the Central Processing Unit
1. The brain [1]
2. [6]

Device	Input	Output
Keyboard	✓	
Printer		✓
Monitor		✓
Webcam	✓	
Sensor	✓	
Speakers		✓

3. The ALU [1]
4. The cache [1]
5. This controls the flow of data around the system [1]
6. This means that both the computer program [1] and the data it processes are stored in memory [1]
7. Memory Address Register [1] and Memory Data Register [1]

8. Accumulator [1]
9. The program counter [1]
10. The 1940s [1]

Systems Architecture
1. Fetch – The instruction is brought from memory
   Decode – The instruction is decoded to enable it to be understood
   Execute – The instruction is carried out [3]
2. GHz [1]
3. 4 [1]
4. Data bottleneck [1]
5. The L1 cache [1]
6. Two billion [1]
7. Being able to carry out more than one task at the same time [1]
8. Any three of the following: DVD player [1]; washing machine [1]; dishwasher [1]; home cinema system [1]; microwave [1] (or similar)
9. Examples include:
   a) Wi-Fi connectivity [1]; backlighting [1]; speaker control [1]; Internet browsing [1]
   b) Program control [1]; temperature sensor [1]; door lock control [1]

Memory
1. Random access memory [1] and read-only memory [1]
2. RAM [1]
3. ROM [1]
4. Once power is switched off [1] all data stored on volatile memory is lost [1]
5. RAM [1]
6. True [1]
7. Basic input/output system [1]
8. B [1]
9. If the RAM becomes full [1]
10. Because it is based in the hard drive memory [1]
11. False [1]
12. Any two of the following: smartphone [1]; laptop [1]; camera [1]; tablet [1]
13. Durability [1]; small size [1]; speed of access [1]

Storage Types, Devices and Characteristics
1. So that programs do not have to be installed each time that we want to use them [1]
2. Magnetically [1]; optically [1]; electronically [1]
3. GB [1]
4. True [1]
5. KB, MB, GB, TB [1]
6. Capacity [1]; speed [1]; portability [1]; durability [1]; reliability [1]; cost [1]
7. DVD [1]
8. SSD (flash) storage [1]
9. Any two of the following: fast read/write access [1]; no moving parts [1]; small size [1]
10. The lifespan of the device or method [1] and advances in storage technology [1]
11. Magnetic storage [1]

Pages 18–19
1. Any five of the following: virus; worm; Trojan; spyware; adware; ransomware; pharming
2. The technique of watching a user at an ATM (cash) machine (or similar) and recording their PIN details
3. Keep one hand over the other as you type to shield your PIN details; keep your body close to the ATM machine, blocking the keyboard from view
4. Denial of service attack

Pages 20–21
1. Digital telephones; Wi-FI networking; streaming music and video services; email services
2. If hackers acquire the password, they could access multiple systems
3. To test the security of its system to find any weaknesses before others find them

Pages 22–23
1. Windows 10, macOS, Unix, Chrome OS, BeOS, MS-Dos, Linux, Ubuntu
2. Faster: an incremental backup backs up files that have changed since the last backup rather than backing up the whole system
3. Examples of OSs: Windows, Mac, Linux; examples of applications: office programs, photo editing, games, music management; examples of utilities: anti-virus, adware removers, disk defragmentation, file converters

The Purpose and Function of the Central Processing Unit
1. Input [1]; process [1]; output [1]
2. Output [1]
3. The cache [1]
4. Arithmetic logic unit [1]
5. The control unit [1]
6. The bus [1]
7. Memory Data Register [1]
8. An instruction or piece of data fetched from memory is stored in the MDR temporarily until used [1]
9. The ALU [1]
10. The MAR [1]

Systems Architecture
1. Execute [1]
2. True [1]
3. Decoded [1]
4. The L1 cache [1]; very fast [1]; slower [1]; more efficient [1]
5. True [1]

6. Clock speed [1]; cache size [1]; number of cores [1]
7. a) 6 [1]
   b) 4 [1]
   c) 1 [1]
   d) 2 [1]
   e) 8 [1]
8. A computer system with a specific function [1] within a larger system [1]
9. The pump control system can be removed and replaced without replacing the whole dishwasher [1]

Memory
1. B [1]
2. DRAM [1]; SRAM [1]
3. ROM [1]
4. Data written to it is stored permanently [1]
5. RAM is much quicker to access [1]; the CPU can quickly identify memory locations in RAM [1]
6. ROM [1]
7. RAM [1]
8. The system hard drive [1]
9. It is both programmable and erasable [2]
10. BIOS instructions can be rewritten at a later date, allowing for upgrades [1]
11. User expandable memory is cheaper than factory-installed storage [1]; customers can specify their own storage requirements [1]

Storage Types, Devices and Characteristics
1. CPU [1]; motherboard [1]
2. Solid-state drive [1]
3. 8 [1]
4. 1,000,000 [1]
5. kilo – thousand
   mega – million
   giga – billion
   tera – trillion [4]
6. Blu-ray [1]
7. Magnetic storage [1]
8. Advantages (any two of the following): cheap [1]; portable [1]; widely available [1]. Disadvantages (any two of the following): easily damaged [1]; limited capacity [1]; correct player needed [1]
9. CD [1]; DVD [1]; Blu-ray [1]
10. Data can be transferred to and from the SSD more quickly [1]
11. When using such a device while walking or running, the complex drive would eventually become damaged [1]

Pages 28–31 **Practice Questions** System Security and Software

Common System Threats
1. Any three of the following: usernames [1]; passwords [1]; dates of birth [1]; family details [1]; pet names [1]; locations [1]; bank account details [1]
2. Password [1]; social network [1]; bank [1]; hacker [1]; accounts [1]
3. Malicious software [2]
4. Trojan or Trojan horse software [1]
5. Worm [1]
6. To lock a user out of a system or their files [1] until a fee is paid to the creator of the malware [1]
7. Email [1]; text messaging [1]; phone calls [1]

8. Watching a user at an ATM machine [1] and recording their PIN details [1]
9. It is carried out face to face [1]
10. It repeatedly [1] tries different usernames and passwords to attempt to access a system [1]
11. Denial [1] of service [1]
12. Users can bring in unsecure files [1]; important files can be released onto external networks [1]

Threat Prevention
1. To ensure that it is up to date with all of the latest threats [1]
2. Encryption [1]
3. Firewall [1]
4. Network policies – Rules all users within a large network must follow to protect security
   Network forensics – Monitors and records network traffic in case of any network attacks
   Penetration testing – Searching for potential weaknesses in a system that could be exploited [3]
5. They might have different roles with different levels of security access [1]
6. The users [1]
7. B [1]; D [1]

System Software
1. Hardware [1]; software [1]; user [1]
2. Graphical user interface [1]
3. Any four of the following: scanner [1]; printer [1]; speaker [1]; webcam [1]; microphone [1]; graphics tablet [1]
4. A mouse [1]
5. It may stop working [1]
6. Supports [1]; system security [1]; management [1]
7. The reduction in size of a file so that it takes up less disk space [1]
8. An incremental backup creates a backup copy of only the files that have changed since the last backup [1]
9. Defragmentation [1]
10. Any three of the following: word processing software [1]; games software [1]; spreadsheet software [1]; graphics or photo editing software [1]; data modelling software [1]

Pages 32–39 **Revise Questions**

Pages 32–33
1. To connect LANs in different banks around the world
2. The spread of viruses disguised as legitimate software or media; users not realizing that their files are being shared
3. a) Quality of transmission media
   b) Interference from external sources
   c) A large number of users on the same network

Pages 34–35
1. A router
2. The Domain Name Server or Service (DNS)
3. a) Sharing files
   b) Collaborative working
   c) Accessing remote files
   d) Playing multiplayer games
   e) Using online or browser-based software

Pages 36–37
1. Each device in the network is connected to every other device in the network
2. The network will fail
3. Any four of the following: router, switch, hub, desktop computer, network printer, tablet, smartphone

Pages 38–39
1. Transport layer and Internet (or network) layer
2. IMAP

Pages 40–43 **Practice Questions** System Security and Software

Common System Threats
1. Home life [1]; education [1]; workplace [1]
2. Your personal files may be copied to the creator [1]; your keystrokes may be recorded, giving away usernames and passwords [1]
3. Pharming [1]
4. Virus [1]
5. It constantly displays targeted advertising [1] and redirects search requests without permission [1]
6. Phishing [1]
7. Any one of the following: they may not have been informed about computer scams [1]; they may not have much computer experience [1]
8. Any two of the following: at a petrol station [1]; at a shop till [1]; in a restaurant [1]; at an office computer [1]
9. Any three of the following: usernames [1]; passwords [1]; personal details [1]; PIN details [1]; bank or credit card numbers [1]
10. A ransom or demand for payment [1]; a change in the policies of the organization targeted [1]
11. Structured [1] Query [1] Language [1]
12. Commands written in SQL are used [1] instead of usernames and passwords [1] to access and steal private information [1]

Threat Prevention
1. Any three of the following: Trojan [1]; spyware [1]; adware [1]; worms [1]; viruses [1]
2. Hardware based [1]
3. To prevent message data being intercepted [1] and used for criminal purposes [1]
4. Any three of the following: the use of personal devices [1]; acceptable network use [1]; password privacy [1]; data backup procedures [1]
5. To ensure that customer details are kept secure [1] and to prevent customer details from being used for criminal purposes [1]
6. Files can be copied on to or removed from the network without permission [1] and files may contain malware [1]
7. Reading a file means that it can be viewed only and no changes can be made [1]. Write access allows the file to be edited or changed and resaved [1]

8. It can be forgotten, preventing access **[1]**
9. A **[1]**; F **[1]**
10. If the password is discovered by a hacker, they have less time to access personal data (such as bank details) **[1]**
11. Hackers can use software to automatically try all dictionary words to crack passwords **[1]**

System Software

1. Any three of the following: smartphone **[1]**; desktop computer **[1]**; laptop **[1]**; tablet **[1]**
2. Windows 10 **[1]**, MacOS **[1]**, Unix **[1]**, Chrome OS **[1]**, BeOS **[1]**, MS-Dos **[1]**, Linux **[1]**, Ubuntu **[1]**
3. Command line prompt or interface **[1]**
4. Any two of the following: drag and drop **[1]**; menu systems **[1]**; mouse-controlled cursor **[1]**
5. The ability to have more than one user account on the same computer **[1]**
6. Users can have their own files and folders **[1]** and specified levels of access to programs and settings **[1]**
7. Software applications created by an external organization or programmer but designed to run in conjunction with the OS **[1]**
8. So that if data is accessed, it cannot be understood (because it is in code) **[1]**
9. A previously saved fully working system can be found **[1]** and then restored over the corrupt system, allowing it to run again **[1]**
10. Any three of the following: flash drive **[1]**; portable hard drive **[1]**; optical drive (CD/DVD/Blu-ray) **[1]**; USB memory stick **[1]**; portable solid-state drive (SSD) **[1]**; cloud storage **[1]**
11. Firewall **[1]**; anti-spyware or anti-malware **[1]**
12. A **[1]**

Pages 44–47 Practice Questions Computer Networking

Wired and Wireless Networks 1

1. Any five of the following: laptop **[1]**; smartphone **[1]**; desktop **[1]**; smart TV **[1]**; router **[1]**; tablet **[1]**
2. Local area network **[1]**; wide area network **[1]**
3. The Internet **[1]**
4. Bandwidth **[1]**; external interference **[1]**; the number of users **[1]**
5. A central computer server **[1]** that hosts programs and controls access **[1]** and is connected to a number of low-specification machines **[1]**
6. Peer-to-peer network **[1]**
7. Bits per second **[1]**
8. Any of the following: users may not be aware that other users on the network can access their files **[1]**; malware can be spread between computers **[1]**; users are unaware of other users' locations **[1]**
9. Fibre-optic technology **[1]**

Wired and Wireless Networks 2

1. Network interface controller/card **[1]**
2. Wi-Fi **[1]**; Bluetooth **[1]**; 3G/4G mobile network **[1]**

3. Router **[1]**
4. Media access control **[1]**
5. Domain Name Server **[1]**
6. Virtual network **[1]**
7. Cloud computing **[1]**; Internet **[1]**; remote **[1]**; applications **[1]**
8. HTML **[1]**
9. The web-hosting company rents out web space on its Internet-connected server **[1]** and customers can then upload their web pages, making them accessible online all over the world. **[1]** Other companies are responsible for storing the data so customers must be able to trust them **[1]**

Network Topologies

1. Star **[1]**; mesh **[1]**; bus **[1]**; ring **[1]**
2. Server **[1]**
3. Advantages (any two of the following): the failure of one device, as long as it is not the server, will not affect the rest of the network **[1]**; additional devices can easily be added **[1]**; problems can be found easily **[1]**; data is quickly directed to a specific address by the server **[1]**. Disadvantages: if the server fails, so will the network **[1]**; extensive cabling and knowledge are required **[1]**
4. False **[1]**
5. If a device fails, the connection around the network is broken **[1]**
6. Bus network **[1]**
7. Because each device is connected to every other device **[1]**
8. A device at an intersection/connection point within a network **[1]**

Protocols and Layers

1. 2.4 GHz **[1]**; 5 GHz **[1]**
2. It is out of date **[1]**; it can be easily hacked **[1]**
3. Any two of the following: Ethernet **[1]**; TCP/IP **[1]**; HTTP **[1]**; HTTPS **[1]**; FTP **[1]**; POP **[1]**; IMAP **[1]**; SMTP **[1]**
4. Packet switching **[1]**
5. HTTPS **[1]**
6. FTP **[1]**
7. Application layer – Data relevant to web browsers and email clients
   Transport layer – Ensures that data is correctly sent and received between network hosts
   Internet (or network) layer – Communicates the IP addresses of devices between routers
   Data link layer – Concerned with physical data transfer over cables **[4]**
8. Ethernet cable **[1]**
9. Transmission Control Protocol/Internet Protocol **[1]**

Pages 48–53 Revise Questions

Pages 48–49

1. Examples:
   a) Use of social network posts
   b) GPS tagging of photos
   c) Use of online shopping services
   d) Unencrypted emails
   e) Mobile phone signal locations
   f) Accessing open Wi-Fi networks
2. a) In high-angle camera fire and rescue services

   b) For video recording of extreme sports
   c) In film-making – much cheaper than filming from a helicopter
3. Risks of being infected with malware from websites; breaking copyright law without knowledge; original content creators not being paid for their efforts

Pages 50–51

1. a) By reducing the amount of computer hardware e-waste disposed of in landfill sites
   b) Older machines with a lower specification can still be used in developing countries
   c) By reducing the use of rare metals and minerals
2. Potential for accidents if a computer fails; questions about who would be responsible in the case of accidents; how standard and driverless cars will exist together on the same roads; and what the charging and power requirements of driverless cars will be
3. Any five of the following: copper; gold; platinum; silver; tungsten; neodymium; terbium; dysprosium

Pages 52–53

1. Computer Misuse Act 1990
2. Freedom of Information Act 2000
3. Data Protection Act 1998

Pages 54–57 Review Questions Computer Networking

Wired and Wireless Networks 1

1. Any two of the following: to enable access to apps **[1]**; to enable the downloading of programme guides **[1]**; to obtain firmware updates **[1]**; to enable connection to streaming services **[1]**
2. Switch **[1]**
3. False **[1]**
4. Client–server network **[1]**
5. Microwave **[1]**
6. Any two of the following: a user account can be managed remotely **[1]**; the processing workload is reduced **[1]**; backups can be created from a central source **[1]**
7. Classroom resources and teaching materials can be shared **[1]**
8. A user on the network can access the contents of any other user's computer on the same network **[1]**

Wired and Wireless Networks 2

1. Switch **[1]**; router **[1]**
2. True **[1]**
3. Wireless access point **[1]**
4. Bluetooth **[1]**
5. 1990s **[1]**
6. Router **[1]**
7. Data can be sent over much longer distances **[1]**
8. Without access to the Internet the business cannot access its files **[1]**; all computer devices within the business must have Internet connectivity **[1]**
9. Websites are given user-friendly text addresses rather than a multi-digit IP address **[1]**

Network Topologies

1. Mesh network [1]
2. Star network [1]
3. D [1]
4. Star – If the server fails then the whole network will collapse
   Mesh – Managing the network requires a high level of network expertise
   Ring – Data travels quickly, in one direction, but if one node fails the network fails
   Bus – If the central spine fails then so does the network [4]
5. Router [1]

Protocols and Layers

1. It prevents interference from other local wireless networks [1]
2. 14 at 2.4 GHz [1]; 25 at 5 GHz [1]
3. WPA2 [1]
4. Hexadecimal [1]
5. IP address [1]
6. IMAP [1]
7. Application layer [1]
8. Wi-Fi certified [1]
9. Any two of the following: splitting the file into pieces [1] and allowing each piece to take any available route [1] prevents data traffic congestion or bottlenecks [1]
10. When a static IP address is assigned to a computer by an external provider it is fixed and cannot be changed [1]. A dynamic address is usually assigned within a network and can change as new devices are added or if the network is restarted [1]

Pages 58–61 **Practice Questions**
Ethical, Legal, Cultural and Environmental Concerns

Ethical and Legal Concerns

1. Global Positioning System [1]
2. Cookies are accessible data files, saved on our computer [1], that contain our Internet history [1]
3. What are social networks doing with all the data they hold about us? [1]; Should mobile phones and/or internet records be checked by government agencies? [1]; Should our internet access be more restricted? [1]
4. Robots can operate 24/7 [1]; tasks are repeated precisely [1]
5. The ability to sell products across the world [1]; the ability to hide one's identity [1]
6. Copyright laws [1]
7. To prevent acts of terrorism [1]
8. Those creating abusive messages and material can be tracked back to their own computer [1]
9. Fun: filming active sports (or similar) [1]; commercial: potential delivery system [1]; government: surveillance or pilotless combat [1]
10. Ability to do repetitive tasks without tiring [1]; ability to work 24/7 [1]
11. Personal information can be used to access other accounts [1] and guess our passwords [1]

Cultural and Environmental Concerns

1. Any three of the following: communication [1]; health [1]; transport [1]; education [1]; leisure activities [1]
2. Any two of the following: lack of access to technology [1]; financial constraints – being unable to buy the latest technology [1]; geographical constraints – restricted Internet access in rural areas [1]
3.

Impact	Positive	Negative
Replacement of physical media with downloads.	✓	
Cost of the transportation of raw and synthetic materials for the production of smart devices.		✓
The development of renewable energy sources.	✓	

[3]

4. It can be accessed anywhere in the world by anyone with an Internet connection [1]
5. Because of the wide range of materials used to create them, which often includes rare elements [1]
6. Benefits: fewer accidents, as traffic flow is controlled [1]; driver mistakes are reduced [1]; efficient navigation reduces travel time [1]. Drawbacks: lack of customer trust [1]; potential for high-speed crashes [1]; complexity and increased cost [1]
7. Making the player feel as if they are part of the game [1]
8. Any one of the following: lack of telephone line access [1]; lack of mains electricity [1]; lack of mobile phone coverage [1]
9. Any two of the following: saving trees [1], which help to reduce greenhouse gases [1]; reduction of paper transportation costs [1]

Computer Science Legislation

1. Any three of the following: data should be fairly and lawfully processed [1]; data must be obtained and used only for specified purposes [1]; data shall be adequate, relevant and not excessive [1]; data should be accurate and kept up to date [1]; data should not be kept for longer than necessary [1]; access must be granted to data subjects to enable them to check and correct their entries [1]; data must be kept safe and secure [1]; data should not be transferred outside the EEA to a country without adequate protection legislation [1]
2. Creative Commons Licensing [1]
3. That there is no legal owner of the material and it can be used for any purpose [1]
4. Copyright Designs and Patents Act 1988 [1]

5. Hacking [1]
6. False [1]
7. Freedom of Information Act 2000 [1]
8. Any person whose details are held on an organization's computer system [1]
9. Computer Misuse Act 1990 [1]
10. Making sure that the original creator of a piece of work has been acknowledged [1]
11. True [1]

Pages 62–69 **Revise Questions**

Pages 62–63
1. A binary search
2. Abstraction

Pages 64–65
1. The act of repeating any process until a specified result is achieved
2. Examples include days of the week, hours/minutes in a day, pi and degrees in a circle

Pages 66–67
1. A single equals sign is used for the definition of variables
2. x = 2
3. False

Pages 68–69
1. An OR gate
2. A NOT gate
3. 8

Pages 70–73 **Practice Questions**
Ethical, Legal, Cultural and Environmental Concerns

Ethical and Legal Concerns

1. Ethical use of computer technology means trying to cause no harm to others [1] and acting in a morally correct way to improve society [1]
2. So that they can use our location to customize the application or suggest local services [1]
3. The application may pass our contact details on to third parties [1]
4. Positive: jobs are created to build and program the robots [1]; negative: robots may replace manual labourers [1]
5. They must constantly train staff to try to keep up with the latest cybercrime methods [1]
6. Illegal music and video streaming sites are easy to access [1] without parental knowledge or knowledge of copyright laws [1]
7. Any two of the following: it is too easy to access illegal or copyrighted material [1]; we can become victims of hackers and malware without our knowledge [1]; there are scams and false information on the Internet [1]; there is a lack of age-related content controls [1]

Cultural and Environmental Concerns

1. Positive: jobs can be applied for quickly and around the world from home [1]; negative: those without reliable Internet access or the ability to use the Internet miss out [1]
2. Any three of the following: reductions in the use of paper [1]; reductions in material costs from the use of

downloads instead of physical media [1]; mobile and home working reduces transportation costs [1]; smarter devices control their energy usage to meet our needs, reducing wastage [1]; the development of increasingly efficient renewable energy production [1]
3. Either of the following: they did not grow up with computer technology [1]; computer technology was not part of their education, unlike children today [1]
4. Lack of power and/or infrastructure [1]; lack of Internet connectivity [1]
5. Any computer-related technology that cannot be recycled easily [1]
6. One teacher can stream a single lesson to multiple classrooms at once [1]
7. Virtual reality headset [1]
8. Users do not keep their devices for their full lifetime [1]; the manufacturing of new devices increases energy consumption and the release of greenhouse gases [1]
9. Doctors can share results and ideas all around the world, allowing them to pool their knowledge [1]

Computer Science Legislation
1. A request is made to a government minister to release details about their expenses – Freedom of Information Act 2000
   An employee takes a company's customer database to a new company – Data Protection Act 1998
   An online email server is hacked and personal messages are stolen – Computer Misuse Act 1990 [3]
2. Creative Commons Licensing allows the creators of original material to share their work but with conditions attached [1]
3. Open source software can be shared and edited without limits [1], whereas proprietary software is owned by its creator and can be used only with permission or through a licence [1]
4. Films [1]; music [1]; games [1]; books [1]
5. The original creator must be credited if a piece of work is copied or used [1] and the piece of work cannot be used to generate money commercially [1]
6. Computer Misuse Act 1990 [1]
7. Companies should have updated their records for the previous family [1] and deleted them if they were no longer required [1]
8. Identify any copyright terms in relation to the images [1] and contact the owner, if required, to gain permission to use the images [1]

Pages 74–77 Practice Questions
Algorithms and Computational Logic

Algorithms and Flow Diagrams
1. An algorithm is a step-by-step sequence of instructions [1] to solve a problem or carry out a task [1]
2. Sequence – Tasks are carried out step by step in sequence
   Iteration – Certain tasks are repeated until a certain condition is met

Selection – A decision needs to be made before the next step can be carried out [3]
3. Decomposition [1]; abstraction [1]; pattern recognition [1]
4. Linear search [1], as it examines each value in turn until a match is found [1]
5. The first two values in a list are compared with each other [1] and the larger is placed first in the list [1]. The next pair of values is then checked, swapped if required, and so on, until the values are listed in descending order [1]
6. Merge sort [1]; insertion sort [1]
7. Diamond [1]
8. [5]

Shape	Description
(rounded rectangle)	Used at the start or end point of a flow diagram.
(parallelogram)	Used to represent the input or output of data in a process.
(diamond)	Used when a decision or choice must be made.
(rectangle)	A process symbol, used to indicate a process or computational task being carried out.
(subroutine box)	Used to represent a sub-routine that can be called at various points of an algorithm.

Pseudocode 1
1. Pseudocode uses simple English terminology and syntax [1]. It is not designed to be run by a computer and so simple errors are allowed [1]
2. if – Used in a question, as part of a decision process
   else – To provide a response if a statement is not met
   then – To provide a response if a statement is met
   while – A loop with a condition set at the start
   print – To display a response on screen to the user
   input – Requires an entry from the user in response to a question
   for – Used to create a counting loop [7]
3. So that variables and functions are easily identifiable [1]
4.

Value	Variable	Constant
numberCars = 19	✓	
daysofYear = 365		✓
hoursinDay = 24		✓
penWidth = 5	✓	

[4]

5. It allows personal notes to be added to coding to explain thinking [1]
6. Example:

```
colour = input("What is your favourite colour?")
print(colour,", that's my favourite colour too, good choice")
```
[2]

7. Example:

```
while answer! = "7"
    answer = input("How many days are in a week?")
endwhile
do
    answer = input("How many days are in a week?")
until answer == "7"
```
[4]

Pseudocode 2
1. a) Exactly equal to [1]
   b) Not equal to [1]
   c) Less than [1]
   d) Less than or equal to [1]
   e) Greater than [1]
   f) Greater than or equal to [1]
2. MOD (modulus) [1]
3. Exponentiation [1]; 27 [1]
4. AND [1]; OR [1]; NOT [1]
5. DIV [1]
6. a) 24 [1]
   b) 729 [1]
   c) 1 [1]
   d) 1 [1]
7. Example:

```
low = 15
high = 25
temp = input("What is the temperature outside?")
if temp > = low OR <= high
    print("Perfect!")
else
    print("Not quite right")
endif
```
[4]

Computational Logic

1. Transistor [1]

2.

AND Gate

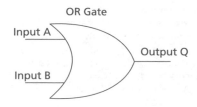
Input A
Input B
Output Q

OR Gate

Input A
Input B
Output Q

NOT Gate

Input A
Output Q

[3]

3. [4]

Inputs		Output
A	B	Q
0	0	0
1	0	1
0	1	1
1	1	1

4. a)

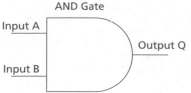
A
B
C
X

Inputs			Output	[8]
A	B	C	X	
0	0	0	0	
0	1	0	0	
1	0	0	0	
1	1	0	0	
0	0	1	0	
0	1	1	0	
1	0	0	0	
1	1	1	1	

b)

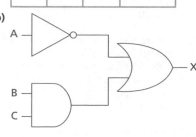
A
B
C
X

Inputs			Output	[8]
A	B	C	X	
0	0	0	0	
0	0	1	0	
0	1	0	0	
0	1	1	1	
1	0	0	1	
1	0	1	1	
1	1	0	1	
1	1	1	1	

5.

Inputs			Output	[8]
A	B	C	X	
0	0	0	1	
0	0	1	1	
0	1	0	1	
0	1	1	1	
1	0	0	0	
1	0	1	1	
1	1	0	1	
1	1	1	1	

Pages 78–87 Revise Questions

Pages 78–79
1. Real (or float) data
2. Concatenation
3. Write mode

Pages 80–81
1. A primary key
2. 1
3. SELECT firstName FROM addressBook

Pages 82–83
1. Time and avoiding repetitive code
2. A two-dimensional array
3. Functions

Pages 84–85
1. To allow for specific functionality for each user and to prevent clashes caused by multiple logins
2. Syntax error and logic error

Pages 86–87
1. Machine code
2. Interpreter
3. Examples include Java, JavaScript, Visual Basic, C++, Ruby, BASIC and Python

Pages 88–91 Review Questions
Algorithms and Computational Logic

Algorithms and Flow Diagrams
1. Iteration [1]
2. Decomposition – Breaking tasks into smaller tasks that are easier to understand
   Abstraction – The removal of unwanted or unnecessary information from a task
   Pattern recognition – Being able to identify patterns in data and to build efficient algorithms [3]

3. The sequence is not ordered [1]
4. Data is repeatedly split into two halves [1] until each list contains only one item [1]. The items are then merged back together into the order required [1]
5. To represent the flow and direction of data [1]
6. Sub-routine [1]
7. Input/output symbol (parallelogram) [1]

Pseudocode 1
1. for [1]
2. Naming conventions [1]
3. Constant [1]
4. 100 [1]
5. // This closes the program [1]
6. It asks for an answer to a multiple choice question [1]. If no answer is provided and the return key is pressed, the program will ask again for an answer [1]. The sequence will stop when A, B or C is entered [1]

Pseudocode 2
1. Comparison [1]
2. Boolean operators – Used to define relationships using logical operators
   Arithmetic operators – Used for mathematical calculations in pseudocode
   Comparison operators – Used to test the relationship between two values [3]
3. The single equals sign = is used to define a variable [1]. The double equals sign == means exactly equal to when testing relationships [1]
4. a) < [1]
   b) > [1]
   c) <= [1]
   d) >= [1]
5. MOD [1]
6. OR [1]
7. Some keywords, functions and symbols are defined differently in different languages [1]

Computational Logic
1. NOT gate [1]
2.

Inputs		Output
A	B	Q
0	0	0
1	0	0
0	1	0
1	1	1

[4]

3. B and C are inputs and X is an output [2]
4. Turned on [1]
5. 16 [1]
6. OR gate [1]
7. Off and on, respectively [2]

Pages 92–95 Practice Questions
Programming Techniques, Programs, Translators and Languages

Programming Techniques 1
1. Integer – A whole number with no decimal point
   Boolean – Digital data – can present only two values

Real (or float) – All numbers, including those with a decimal points
Character – A single letter, number or symbol
String – A collection of alphanumeric data characters and symbols **[5]**
2. Real data **[1]**
3. The conversion of one data type into another **[1]**
4. To convert the number 42 into a string **[1]**
5. Quotation marks **[1]**
6. Concatenation **[1]**
7. openRead will simply open an existing file in read-only mode **[1]**, whereas openWrite will create a new file or overwrite an existing file **[1]**
8.
```
endOfFile()
```
[1]
9. It would open the file called petNames.txt **[1]**, replace the contents with the name Poppy **[1]** and close the file **[1]**

Programming Techniques 2
1. Data **[1]**; tables **[1]**; fields **[1]**; records **[1]**; primary key **[1]**
2. A flat-file database has only one table **[1]**, whereas a relational database has multiple databases, linked together by a common key field **[1]**
3. Structured Query Language **[1]**
4. Search for a student with an examination score of greater than 80 **[1]** and display their surname **[1]** from a database called Classlist **[1]**
5.
```
SELECT firstName
FROM Classlist
WHERE examScore = 55
```
[1]
[1]
[1]

Programming Techniques 3
1. An array is a data structure for storing groups within a program **[1]**, meaning that several pieces of data can be stored under one name or variable **[1]**
2. Two-dimensional array **[1]**
3. Parameters **[1]**
4. Procedures **[1]** and functions **[1]**

Producing Robust Programs
1. Use of authentication to check the identity of a user **[1]**; use of passwords to prevent unauthorized access **[1]**; user access linked to usernames/passwords **[1]**; plan for users making mistakes **[1]**
2. To ensure that it is easy to understand by other programmers **[1]** and straightforward to edit at a later date **[1]**
3. Use of indentation **[1]**, variables **[1]** and sub-routines **[1]**
4. Performance testing considers the impact on system resources of normal use of a program **[1]**, whereas load/stress testing attempts to crash the program and system by having multiple users access it at the same time **[1]**
5. Syntax error **[1]**
6. Normal data – Acceptable data likely to be input into the program
Extreme data – Values at the limit of what a program can handle
Erroneous data – Values the program should not accept or process **[3]**
7. A test plan should spot program errors

and potential user problems **[1]** before the program is released commercially to help prevent poor customer reviews **[1]**
8. Any five of the following: test number **[1]**; test description/reason **[1]**; test data to be used **[1]**; expected outcome **[1]**; actual outcome **[1]**; further action if required **[1]**

Translators and Facilities of Languages
1. Humans use high-level languages to write programs, which must then be translated before a computer can understand them **[1]**, whereas low-level languages are much closer to a format that a computer can understand **[1]**
2. Binary **[1]**
3. Machine code **[1]**
4. It translates any programming language **[1]** other than machine code into a format that a computer can understand **[1]**
5. Assemblers – Required to convert low-level languages, such as assembly language, into instructions
Compilers – Used to read high-level languages and convert programs as a whole into machine code programs
Interpreters – Examine high-level language files one line at a time and convert each instruction into compatible machine code instructions **[3]**
6. Interpreter **[1]**
7. Integrated development environment **[1]**
8. Code editor **[1]**; carrying out error diagnostics **[1]**; providing a run-time environment **[1]**; translator **[1]**
9. Code editor or text editor **[1]**

Pages 96–103 **Revise Questions**
Pages 96–97
1. 4
2. To create an 8-bit (1-byte) character set
3. 256

Pages 98–99
1. 11000100
2. Any binary value greater than 255
3. 2

Pages 100–101
1. 35
2. 314
3. The last digit on the right

Pages 102–103
1. 2.2 MB
2. MP3
3. Lossless compression, to maintain quality as high as possible

Pages 104–107 **Practice Questions**
Programming Techniques, Programmes, Translators and Languages

Programming Techniques 1
1. a) int **[1]**
   b) bool **[1]**
   c) real (or float) **[1]**
   d) char **[1]**
   e) str **[1]**
2. Character **[1]**
3. Casting or typecasting **[1]**

4.
```
string1 = "Good morning
Dave"
print(string1)
```
[1]
[1]
5. Concatenation **[1]**
6. a) 12 (number of characters) **[1]**
   b) HELLO WORLD! **[1]**
   c) The third character 'l' **[1]**
7. It will overwrite the contents of the file **[1]**

Programming Techniques 2
1. identNumber **[1]** because the primary key needs to be unique **[1]**
2. A common key field **[1]**
3. This is a language **[1]** designed to create, edit and search databases **[1]**
4. Ascending order **[1]**

Programming Techniques 3
1. Example:
```
array season[4]
season[0] = "Winter"
season[1] = "Spring"
season[2] = "Summer"
season[3] = "Autumn"
```
[2]
2. Example:
```
temp = ["21", "24", "26", "28"]
```
[3]
3. Example:
```
carSurvey [3,3]
carSurvey = [[Cars,
"6","9"],[Bikes, "4","3"],
[Vans, "6","6"]]
```
[4]
4. Row 0, column 2: 9 **[1]**
5. A procedure is a named group of instructions that is used as required to complete a set task, whereas a function is a group of instructions designed to return a value that can be processed easily **[2]**

Producing Robust Programs
1. Defensive design **[1]**
2. Program maintainability **[1]**
3. D **[1]**
4. c) **[1]**; it should be clear to the reader what the content of the variable will be **[1]**
5. Iterative testing **[1]**; final testing **[1]**; usability testing **[1]**; security testing **[1]**; load/stress testing **[1]**
6. Syntax error **[1]**
7. a) 10 **[1]**
   b) 1 or 12 **[1]**
   c) 15 **[1]**
8. Expected outcome is what you imagine should happen if the program is run, based on your planning **[1]**. Actual outcome is what happens when the program is run for the first time **[1]**

Translators and Facilities of Languages
1. Because low-level languages are much closer to direct instructions that a computer can understand, whereas high-level languages are written by humans and contain keywords and syntax that programmers understand **[1]**

2. Used to read high-level languages and convert programs as a whole into machine code programs [1]
3. Because a compiler converts a whole program at once [1]
4. Assembler [1]
5. Programs can be written and tested [1] without potentially causing damage to complex machinery [1]
6. Run-time environment [1]

Pages 108–111 **Practice Questions** Data Representation

Units and Formats of Data
1. B [1]
2. 32 bits [1]
3. 6 GB [1]
4. Designed to convert alphanumeric characters [1] typed into a computer into a usable binary equivalent [1]
5. American Standard Code for Information Interchange [1]
6. 128 [1]
7. The original ASCII binary equivalent was a 7-bit code with 128 possible characters [1]; an extra zero (bit) was added to every binary sequence to create an 8-bit (1-byte) character set [1]
8. Unicode [1]

Converting Data 1
1. a) Base 10 [1]
   b) Base 2 [1]
2. a) 1 [1]
   b) 255 [1]
   c) 181 [1]
   d) 51 [1]
   e) 85 [1]
   f) 240 [1]
3. 11101000 [1]
4. 11111111 [1] because all 8 bits have been used [1]
5. An error caused by any binary value greater than 255 or 11111111 [1]
6. a) Multiply by 2 [1]
   b) Divide by 2 [1]

Converting Data 2
1. 0, 1, 2, 3, 4, 5, 6, 7, 8, 9, A, B, C, D, E, F [1]
2. To enable them to express large binary numbers [1]
3. To prevent the duplication of numbers [1]
4. a) 31 [1]
   b) AD [1]
   c) 7E [1]
   d) E1 [1]
5. a) 109 [1]
   b) 59 [1]
   c) 117 [1]
6. Check digit [1]

Audio/Visual Formats and Compression
1. Metadata – Additional information saved within the image file
   Colour depth – The number of bits per pixel
   Resolution – The number of pixels used to create an image [3]
2. 00 [1]; 01 [1]; 10 [1]; 11 [1]
3. 1,000,500 pixels [1]

4. 16 bits [1]
5. 15,876 MB [1]
6. A higher sample rate means that more bits are used to encode the sample, which will increase the file size [1]
7. Original fine detail can be lost if compression settings are too high [1]
8. Any three of the following: JPEG [1]; MP3 [1]; GIF [1]; MP4 [1]
9. True [1]

Pages 116–119 **Practice Questions** Data Representation

Units and Formats of Data
1. Around 1 GB (music = 900 MB) [1]
2. C [1]
3. True [1]
4. Extended [1]; 256 [1]; European [1]; accents [1]
5. Unicode was developed as a world industry standard [1] to represent all known languages [1]
6. ASCII coding groups [1]

Converting Data 1
1. Decimal [1]
2. 1, 2, 4, 8, 16, 32, 64, 128 [1]
3. a) 00111100 [1]
   b) 10111101 [1]
   c) 00101000 [1]
   d) 00001011 [1]
   e) Overflow [1]
   f) 01100011 [1]
4. 2 [1]
5. 00001010 [1]; 80 [1] and 10 [1]
6. Because the value 0 is included [1]

Converting Data 2
1. 16 [1]
2. 2 [1]
3. a) 10001011 [1]
   b) 00010001 [1]
   c) 00111111 [1]
   d) 11110010 [1]
4. Any three of the following: in the international ISBN system used to number and catalogue books [1]; bank card numbers [1]; vehicle registration numbers [1]; barcode numbers [1]
5. False [1]
6. a) C7 [1]
   b) 32 [1]
   c) F2 [1]

Audio/Visual Formats and Compression
1. Pixels [1]
2.

0	0	1	1	0	0
0	1	1	1	1	0
1	1	1	1	1	1
1	1	1	1	1	1
0	1	0	0	1	0
1	0	0	1	0	0

[2]

3. Any three of the following: GPS data [1]; camera aperture and shutter speed [1]; date and time that a photograph was taken [1]; data added by the user [1]
4. 256 [1]
5. 0.48 MB [3]

6. Sampling [1]
7. The number of samples taken each second when converting into audio [1]
8. Less storage space required [1]; faster uploading and downloading [1]; online streaming services run more smoothly [1]
9. In lossless compression the original quality of files is preserved [1] when

Pages 120–129 **Mix it Up Questions**

1. 3E to binary = 0011 1110 [1]
   0011 1110 to decimal = 62 [1]
2. Optical [1]; magnetic [1]; solid state [1]
3. Any two of the following: error diagnostics [1]; run-time environment [1]; code editor [1]; translator [1]
4. 01110001 [2], 113 [1]
5. Input signals through pressing the screen [1] and visual output via the screen [1]
6. Any four of the following:
   An instruction is fetched from memory [1]
   The instruction is then decoded [1]
   The decoded instruction is then executed so that the CPU performs continuously [1]
   The process is repeated [1]
   The program counter is incremented [1]
   The instruction is transferred to the MDR [1]
   The address of the instruction to be fetched is placed in the MAR [1]
7. Ransomware locks or disables a computer [1] and payment is demanded to return the computer to normal [1]
8. The Internet is a global network of connected networks [1] and the World Wide Web is a collection of websites hosted on these networks [1]
9.
```
firstName = input("What is
your first name?")          [1]
lastName = input("What is
your last name?")           [1]
    print(firstName + lastName)  [1]
end
```
10. The last digit in a string of numbers is calculated from the other numbers in the string [1] and used to check that a correctly formatted number has been added [1]
11. A compiler translates the program all in one go [1] and an interpreter translates one line at a time [1]
12. Any three of the following: firewall [1]; anti-malware [1]; encryption, [1]; user control [1]; network policies [1]
13. 10111111 [1]
14. IMAP [1]
15. Example answer:
```
function imageCheck           [1]
maxfileSize = 1               [1]
    fileSize = input("Please
    upload file")             [1]
if filesize <= maxfileSize    [1]
    then upload               [1]
else
    print("File too large")   [1]
end
```

16. Bus describes the physical pathway [1] shared by signals to and from components of a computer system such as input and output devices [1]
17. Leaving comments in the code [1]; using clear variable names [1]; naming modules and functions appropriately [1]; using indented code where applicable [1]
18. bit, nibble, byte, MB, GB, PB [1]
19. WEP, WPA, WPA2 [1]; they should use WPA2 [1] as it is the newest [1]
20. Any four of the following: capacity/size [1]; speed [1]; portability [1]; durability [1]; reliability [1]; cost [1]
21. A record is one complete entry in a database [1], whereas a field is one element of a record [1]
22. Virtual memory is created by the CPU on a secondary hard drive [1] when RAM is full [1]
23. Answers similar to the following: Defensive design setting appropriate rules for usernames and passwords [1]; imagining the mistakes users will make [1]; planning incorrect key presses [1]; anticipating unwelcome users trying to access the program [1]
24. Any four of the following: new devices can be added [1]; central management [1]; less chance of data clashes [1]; failing devices will not break the system [1]; data can be targeted at particular devices [1]
25. 57,32,4,5,40,54,2 = starting

32,57	4,5	40,54	2	[1]
4,5	32,57	40,54	2	[1]
2	4,5	32,40,54,57 = finish		

26. An embedded system is a computer system with a specific purpose [1] that is built into a larger system [1]
27. A single equals sign is used to define variables [1] and a double equals sign is used in calculations to represent exactly equal to [1]
28. Any two of the following: cloud-based systems offer additional storage [1], giving more space for student document folders [1]
   Backup systems are often included in cloud-based systems [1], saving time [1]
   Cloud-based systems offer opportunities for home working [1] for students and staff [1]
   Less network expertise needed to use cloud-based systems [1], saving the school money [1]
29. To ensure that there are enough characters available [1] to encode all of the spoken languages in the world [1]
30. The program will have an organised structure [1] and each note can be called upon when required, limiting the repetition of code [1]
31. False [1]
32. HTTPS means that the website has secure encryption [1], protecting his private information when shopping [1]
33. a) memberID [1]
   b) To make sure that each record has a uniquely identifiable field that can be searched for [1]
34. Volatile memory, for example RAM [1], will hold data in memory only if there is a power source [1], whereas non-volatile memory, for example USB storage [1], will keep the contents in memory when power is disconnected [1]
35. Steps: 14,22,12,18 -> 14,12,22,18 -> 12,14,22,18 -> 12,14,18,22 [2]
36. Abstraction is the removal of unwanted or unnecessary information from a task [1], providing focus and clarity [1]
37. Any three of the following: dishwasher [1]; MP3 player [1]; washing machine [1]; mobile phone [1]; home entertainment systems [1]; or similar
38. Unknowingly sharing her files [1]; dangers from malware in downloaded files [1]; downloading copyrighted material [1]
39. Example answers:
   Normal: 04/05/1977 [1]
   Extreme: 01/01/1900 or 31/12/2018 [1]
   Erroneous: 5th June 1969 [1]
40. False [1]
41. Devices are built using rare resources [1] that require additional energy to manufacture [1], creating additional e-waste [1] and toxic waste that can leak into the environment [1]
42. Phishing uses email, text messages and phone calls to impersonate, for example, a financial organisation and ask users to confirm or divulge their personal details [1]. Shouldering is the technique of watching a user at an ATM (cash) machine and recording their PIN details [1]. Blagging is carried out face to face and uses believable scenarios to trick people into giving up their personal information [1]
43. Any three of the following: files on the hard drive are moved [1]; empty spaces are collected together [1]; files are moved to be stored together [1]; fewer disk accesses are needed [1]
44. A denial of service attack tries to flood a website or network with data traffic to bring it to a halt [1]. Such attacks are often used to demand a ransom or a change in policy [1]

Glossary

Abstraction – The removal of unwanted or unnecessary information from a task or problem to provide focus.

Accumulator – Temporarily stores the results of calculations carried out by the ALU.

Adware – A form of spyware designed to automatically open or generate advertisements.

Algorithm – A sequence of step-by-step instructions to solve a problem or carry out a task.

Analogue – A continuous signal that cannot be directly processed by a computer.

Anti-malware – Software designed to stop and remove malicious software from a system.

Application software – Installed into an operating system to actually produce work.

Arguments – The data used by a sub-program.

Arithmetic logic unit (ALU) – The part of the CPU that carries out calculations.

ASCII – A common coding standard of 128 characters for computer manufacturers to share.

Assemblers – A programming translator, used to convert low-level languages into computer instructions.

Assembly language – A low-level programming language.

Attribution – The acknowledgement of an original creator of a piece of work when copying or using it.

Bandwidth – The amount of data that can pass between two network devices per second.

Base 10 – Our standard decimal numbering system.

Base 16 – A number system with 16 characters of numbers and letters, also known as hexadecimal.

Binary – A base 2 number system using two digits: 1 and 0.

Binary search – Looks for a specific value in an ordered list by comparing it to the others around it.

Binary shift – The movement of bits in a binary sequence left and right to represent multiplication and division.

BIOS – Basic input/output system; computer start-up software stored in ROM.

Bit-rate – The number of bits used per second to sample an audio file.

Blagging – The act of using believable scenarios to trick people into giving up personal information.

Blocks – A storage area within a solid-state drive.

Blogs – Websites based around the creation of chronological entries or posts.

Boolean operators – Use of AND, OR and NOT to connect and define relationships between data values or search terms.

Brute force attack – Repeatedly trying different usernames and passwords in an attempt to access a system.

Bubble sort – Repeatedly compares adjacent pairs of values in a list and swaps until all items are in order.

Bus – The connection and transfer of data between devices in a computer system.

C Family – A group of high-level programming languages.

Cache – Quick-to-access memory stored within the CPU.

Casting – In programming, the conversion of one data type into another.

Central processing unit (CPU) – The core of a computer system that processes and controls the flow of data.

Character – A single letter, number or symbol in a program.

Character sets – Alphanumeric characters and symbols, converted into a computer-readable binary equivalent.

Check digit – Used for error detection in identification numbers; the last digit is checked against a criterion.

Client – A computer or workstation that receives information from a central server.

Clock speed – The rate in gigahertz per second at which instructions are processed by the CPU.

Cloud computing – The remote storing and accessibility of files and applications via the Internet.

Colour depth – The number of bits per pixel in an electronic image.

Compliers – Used to read high-level languages and convert programs as a whole into machine code.

Compression – See Data compression.

Concatenation – The adding together of two strings in a program.

Constant – A value that cannot be changed or edited within a running program.

Control unit – The part of the CPU that controls the flow of data both in and around the CPU.

Cookies – Small files stored on computers, accessible by web servers, that contain Internet browsing data.

Copyrighted – The ownership rights of the original creator of any original content.

Cores – The processing units found inside a CPU; each core can carry out a separate task.

Cypher – A method of encrypting or decrypting text.

Data bottlenecks – A problem caused by the processor and bus data transfer running at different speeds.

Data compression – The process of reducing the file size of an electronic file.

Data interception and theft – Intercepting and decoding a message containing sensitive information before it reaches its destination.

Databases – A system for storing large amounts of data, categorized and structured for ease of accessibility.

Decomposition – The process of breaking tasks into smaller tasks that are easier to understand and then solve.

Defragmentation – Re-organising the data on a hard drive to speed up access and free up storage space.

Denary – Also known as decimal, a base 10 number system.

Denial of service attack – Flooding a website or network with data traffic to bring it to a halt.

DNS – Domain Name Server; links the IP address of a computer on a network to a text-based website address.

Drivers – Small programs that control a particular device within a computer system.

Embedded system – A small computer system with a specific purpose that is built into a larger device.

Encryption – The conversion of important data into a form that cannot be read without a key.

Erasable – The ability to remove stored data from a device or chip.

Erroneous (or invalid) data – Incorrect values that the program should not accept or process.

Error diagnostics – Also referred to as debugging tools, used to identify errors in particular lines of code.

Exponentiation – A pseudocode arithmetic operator that assigns one value to the power of another.

Extended ASCII – An extended version of the ASCII system, increasing it to an 8-bit 256-character set.

Extreme (or boundary) data – Values at the limit of what a program should be able to handle.

Fields – A category within a database.

File management – The organisation of files and documents to allow for easy access and retrieval.

Firewalls – Hardware or software designed to protect a system from unauthorized access.

Flat-file database – A database with a single table and no links to other tables.

Flow diagram – Visualizes an algorithm and shows clearly the flow of information.

Full backup – The creation of an exact duplicate of a computer system for security purposes.

Functions – A type of sub-program designed to return a value that the program will use.

GPS – Global Positioning System; a satellite-based navigation system that provides devices with an exact geographical location.

GPS location – A user's current position on the earth calculated using latitude and longitude coordinates.

Graphical user interface – A visual system, often cursor driven, that allows users to access and control a computer system.

Hexadecimal – A base 16 number system of sixteen characters: 0–9 and A–F.

High-level languages – Programming languages, such as Python, containing keywords and syntax that programmers understand.

Hosting – The storing of a website, or a similar file system, on a network computer accessible via the Internet.

Identifier – The name given to a variable so it can be identified in a program.

Immersive – A system designed to engage the user completely in an experience, often using three-dimensional headset technology.

Incremental backup – Making a copy of only the files and documents that have changed since the last backup was made.

Input devices – Devices that provide an input signal into a computer system.

Insertion sort – Repeatedly comparing each item in a list with the previous item and inserting it into the correct position.

Integer – A whole number in a program with no decimal point.

Internet Protocol – A unique identification address assigned to network devices to facilitate Internet connectivity.

Interpreters – Software that converts high-level language file one line at a time into compatible machine code.

Iteration – Repeating a task until a certain condition is met.

Iterative testing – The program cycle of design, development and testing.

Java – A high-level programming language.

LAN – Local area network; computers are connected with the ability to share information in a local area.

Layers – A set of network protocols grouped together with a specific purpose.

Linear search – Compares each value in a list, one at a time, to a required value until a match is made.

Logic diagrams – Graphical representations of simple Boolean operations using gates.

Logic error – A fault in the structure or design of a program.

Lossless compression – The use of an algorithm to compress data but then reconstruct it without data loss.

Lossy compression – File size reduction by permanently removing data such as duplicated data elements.

Low-level languages – Programming languages that are closer to direct instructions that a computer can understand.

Machine code – A low-level programming language that can execute commands directly without any translation.

Malware – Short for malicious software: designed to cause damage or to steal information from the user.

Media access control – A hardwired address assigned to all network devices during manufacture.

Memory Address Register – The location address in memory of the next piece of data or instruction that the CPU needs.

Memory Data Register – A CPU register that stores instructions or pieces of data.

Merge sort – Data is repeatedly split into halves until single items remain, and is then reassembled in order.

Mesh network – A network topology in which every device within the network is connected to every other device.

Metadata – Additional file property data stored within a file, such as the date a photo was taken.

Modulus – A pseudocode arithmetic operator that returns the remainder after a division.

Multimedia – The combination of multiple media elements: text, sound, video, graphics and user interactivity.

Network forensics – Monitors and records network traffic to make sure that any attacks can be analysed.

Network policies – A set of practical rules that all users should follow within a network environment.

Network storage – A secondary storage device that is accessed via network connectivity.

Nibble – 4 bits, half an 8-bit binary sequence.

Non-volatile – Memory that retains its contents even after power is switched off.

Normal data – Acceptable data a program is likely to accept and process.

One-dimensional array – A single list in a program of common elements.

Open source – Software created to be shared openly online at no cost or with no limits on how it can be used.

Operating system – Software designed to manage a computer system, control hardware and allow applications to be run.

Output devices – Devices that receive instructions or commands from a computer system and carry them out.

Overflow error – Occurs when a computer tries to process more bits than it is designed to handle.

Overwritten – Replacing the contents of a file with new data.

Packet switching – Transmitting data packets across multiple networks and reassembling them at the destination.

Parameters – The variables used within a sub-program.

Passwords – Strings of characters, numbers, letters and symbols that allow access to a computer system.

Pattern recognition – The identification of repeating elements or data similarities that can be built into an algorithm.

Penetration testing – The search for vulnerabilities within a system that could be exploited for criminal purposes.

Permissions – Individually set user access rights on a network.

Pharming – Redirecting a user's website request to a fraudulent site, by modifying their DNS entries.

Phishing – Impersonating an organization and asking users to confirm or divulge personal details.

Primary key – A unique identifiable field within a database that cannot be repeated.

Private key – Required to open an encrypted message.

Procedure – A type of sub-program: a set of instructions grouped together and assigned a name.

Program counter – Continuously provides the CPU with the memory address of the next instruction to be carried out.

Proprietary – Owned by the individual or company who created it; permission is usually through a purchased licence.

Protocols – Sets of rules devised for network-compatible devices to allow for effective communication.

Pseudocode – A shared programming language using simple English terms to plan programs.

Public encryption key – Used to encrypt a message to prevent interception; can only be opened with the private key.

Python – A high-level programming language.

Quotient – A pseudocode arithmetic operator that divides but returns only a whole number or integer.

RAM – Random access memory is a temporary area that a computer uses to store data in current use.

Ransomware – Software designed to lock out user access to their system until a ransom is paid to unlock it.

Real (or float) – A program data type; all numbers, including those with a decimal point.

Records – A single row or entry of related data in a database.

Relational database – Multiple databases, linked together by a common key field.

Resolution – The number of pixels used to represent an electronic image.

ROM – Read-only memory provides a computer system with important instructions that do not change.

Routers – Devices that connect networks together and allow communication between them.

Run-time environment – Allows a program to be run and tested within an integrated development environment (IDE).

Sampling – The process of converting analogue into digital.

Sampling frequency – The number of audio samples taken per second when converting analogue into digital.

Secondary storage – Refers to the devices used to store programs, documents and files.

Selection – A decision that needs to be made before the next step can be carried out.

Sequence – Carrying out tasks in a step-by-step sequence.

Server – A dedicated device or software system to provide services or functionality to devices connected to it.

Shouldering – The technique of watching a user at an ATM (cash) machine and recording their PIN details.

Social engineering – Describes a range of methods used by con artists or criminals to access personal information.

Spyware – Malware specifically designed to secretly pass on user information to a third party.

SQL injection – The use of a common database programming language to access and steal information.

Star network – A network topology with a server at the centre and computers with network devices connected around it.

Storage capacities – The amount of data a device can store.

Streaming services – Internet-accessed multimedia content, presented to the user in real time as a constant data stream.

String – A collection of alphanumeric data characters and symbols, usually enclosed in quotation marks.

Structured Query Language – A programming language designed to create, edit and search databases.

Sub-program – A program section that can be called at any time during a larger program to save time/avoid repetition.

Switches – Devices that provide network connectivity between other devices.

Syntax error – A error within a program that breaks the rules or grammar of the language in which it is written.

Test plan – A written plan of program tests, the results and how any errors might be resolved.

Third-party applications – Applications made by an external organisation not connected with the operating system or hardware.

Topology – The logical arrangement or physical structure of computers and network devices.

Transistors – Semiconducting devices used to amplify or switch electronic flow in a circuit.

Translators – Software designed to convert a programming language into machine code.

Trojan – Malware disguised as legitimate software, designed to cause damage or provide access to criminals.

Truth table – The representation of potential inputs and outputs (1s and 0s) in a logic diagram.

Two-dimensional array – An array within which each element contains its own array or list of lists.

Unicode – A character set designed to contain all possible characters from all known languages.

User access levels – Individual permissions for users to limit the information they can access, read or edit.

User management – The management of users on a single computer within the same operating system.

Utility software – Used to carry out specific tasks to support an operating system.

Variable – Part of a program that has been assigned a specific value by the programmer.

Virtual memory – Created by the CPU on the hard drive if RAM becomes full.

Virtual network – A software-managed network created within an existing physical network.

Virus – Malware hidden within another program or file, designed to cause damage to file systems.

Visual Basic – A high-level programming language.

Volatile – Memory that loses all data stored when power is switched off (for example, RAM).

von Neumann architecture – A 'stored program' computer system containing both the computer program and the data it processes.

WAN – Wide area network; created by connecting one LAN to another across a geographical space.

Wi-Fi certified – An international standard for devices meeting industry-agreed network standards.

Worm – Malware with the ability to independently replicate itself and spread throughout a system.

Write – A file handling mode enabling a new file to be created or an existing file to be overwritten.

Index

Collins

OCR GCSE Revision

Computer Science

Computer Science

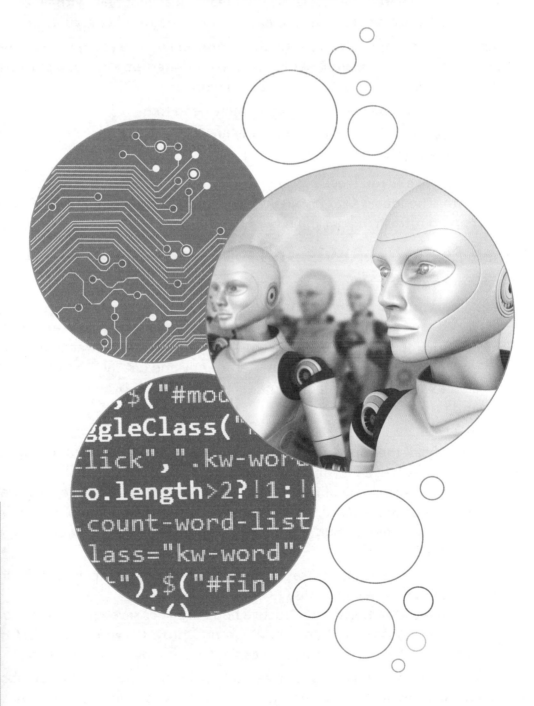

OCR
GCSE

Workbook

Paul Clowrey

Revision Tips

Rethink Revision

Have you ever taken part in a quiz and thought '*I know this*!', but, despite frantically racking your brain, you just couldn't come up with the answer?

It's very frustrating when this happens, but in a fun situation it doesn't really matter. However, in your GCSE exams, it will be essential that you can recall the relevant information quickly when you need to.

Most students think that revision is about making sure you **know** stuff. Of course, this is important, but it is also about becoming confident that you can **retain** that *stuff* over time and **recall** it quickly when needed.

Revision That Really Works

Experts have discovered that there are two techniques that help with all of these things and consistently produce better results in exams compared to other revision techniques.

Applying these techniques to your GCSE revision will ensure you get better results in your exams and will have all the relevant knowledge at your fingertips when you start studying for further qualifications, like AS and A Levels, or begin work.

It really isn't rocket science either – you simply need to:

- **test yourself** on each topic as many times as possible
- **leave a gap** between the test sessions.

It is most effective if you leave a good period of time between the test sessions, e.g. between a week and a month. The idea is that just as you start to forget the information, you force yourself to recall it again, keeping it fresh in your mind.

Three Essential Revision Tips

1. **Use Your Time Wisely**
   - Allow yourself plenty of time.
   - Try to start revising six months before your exams – it's more effective and less stressful.
   - Your revision time is precious so use it wisely – using the techniques described on this page will ensure you revise effectively and efficiently and get the best results.
   - Don't waste time re-reading the same information over and over again – it's time-consuming and not effective!

2. **Make a Plan**
   - Identify all the topics you need to revise (this All-in-One Revision & Practice book will help you).
   - Plan at least five sessions for each topic.
   - One hour should be ample time to test yourself on the key ideas for a topic.
   - Spread out the practice sessions for each topic – the optimum time to leave between each session is about one month but, if this isn't possible, just make the gaps as big as realistically possible.

3. **Test Yourself**
   - Methods for testing yourself include: quizzes, practice questions, flashcards, past papers, explaining a topic to someone else, etc.
   - This All-in-One Revision & Practice book provides seven practice opportunities per topic.
   - Don't worry if you get an answer wrong – provided you check what the correct answer is, you are more likely to get the same or similar questions right in future!

Visit our website to download your free flashcards, for more information about the benefits of these revision techniques, and for further guidance on how to plan ahead and make them work for you.

www.collins.co.uk/collinsGCSErevision

Contents

Systems Architecture, Memory and Storage

The Purpose and Function of the Central Processing Unit

1 Match each term with its definition. [4]

Input	Programmed instructions for a computer with a specific task.
Output	A device that sends information or data to the CPU.
Software	Any physical device that would normally form part of a computer system.
Hardware	A device that receives instructions or data from the CPU.

2 Complete the following diagram using the letters from the box. [4]

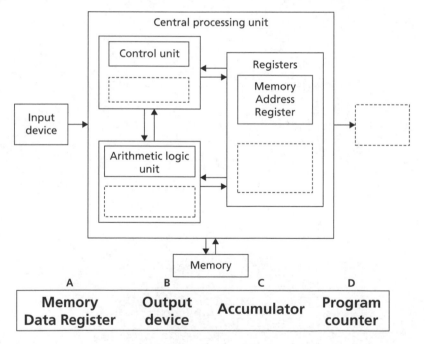

A	B	C	D
Memory Data Register	Output device	Accumulator	Program counter

3 Complete the following sentence.

The pathway shared by signals to and from components of a computer system is known as the . . . [1]

_____

Systems Architecture, Memory and Storage

4 Describe the relationship between the ALU and the accumulator. [2]

5 In von Neumann architecture, what part of the CPU is the program counter found in? [1]

6 In von Neumann architecture, what is meant by the term 'stored program'? [2]

Systems Architecture

1 Define the term 'clock speed'. [1]

2 The clock speed of modern CPUs has slowed in recent years. Instead, CPUs now have multiple cores.

Explain how this change has affected CPU performance. [2]

3 What is the difference between the L1 cache and the L2 cache? [2]

4 A modern washing machine has embedded systems.

Describe **two** benefits that this might offer the manufacturer. [2]

Systems Architecture, Memory and Storage

5 Briefly describe the **four** stages of the fetch–decode–execute cycle. **[4]**

....

....

....

....

6 A computer gamer is concerned that her system is suffering from data bottlenecks.
What does this mean? **[2]**

....

....

....

Memory

1 In a modern computer system, what is the purpose of RAM? **[1]**

....

2 RAM is described as volatile, whereas ROM is described as non-volatile.

a) What do the terms 'volatile' and 'non-volatile' mean? **[2]**

....

....

b) Why is this difference important to computer manufacturers when they are
designing BIOS? **[1]**

....

....

3 When a computer is booted, the BIOS runs.

a) What does the abbreviation BIOS stand for? [1]

....

....

b) State two tasks the BIOS carries out as the computer starts. [2]

....

....

....

4 Virtual memory is created by the operating system when required.

a) Why is virtual memory created? [1]

....

b) Where is virual memory created? [1]

....

c) What problem can virtual memory cause? [1]

....

5 What key benefit does flash memory offer over traditional RAM? [1]

....

6 Some computer designers use flash memory instead of ROM to store system BIOS.
What advantage does this offer? [1]

....

Systems Architecture, Memory and Storage

Storage Types, Devices and Characteristics

1. A teacher is concerned about losing work. She is looking for a secondary storage device that will back up important files.

   List **five** characteristics the teacher should consider when choosing a secondary storage device. **[5]**

   ....

   ....

   ....

   ....

   ....

2. Optical discs are a popular and cheap form of storage.

   a) Name **three** different variations of optical disc. **[3]**

   ....

   ....

   ....

   ....

   ....

   b) State **three** issues that should be considered when using optical discs. **[3]**

   ....

   ....

   ....

   ....

   ....

Systems Architecture, Memory and Storage

3 After many years of using his 120 GB MP3 player, Frank decides to upgrade to a 64 GB flash-based model.

Describe **one** advantage that each device has over the other. **[2]**

....

....

4 Why would an optical drive not be suitable as the main storage for a laptop? **[2]**

....

....

5 Describe **two** characteristics of magnetic storage that prevent it from being used in mobile devices such as smartphones and action cameras. **[2]**

....

....

....

6 Technology experts often warn users to think about the lifespan of storage media when considering backup storage solutions.

Describe **one** way a user can prevent their current backup storage solution becoming outdated. **[1]**

....

....

System Security and Software

Common System Threats

1 Online shopping sites and social networks are often the focus of online attacks designed to steal personal information.

State **four** pieces of information that cyber-criminals would consider valuable. **[4]**

....

....

....

....

2 A virus scan on an infected computer lists the presence of both a worm and a virus. What is the difference between a worm and a virus? **[2]**

....

....

....

3 Match each term with its definition. **[3]**

Pharming		Installed by a user who thinks it is a legitimate piece of software when it is, in fact, malware.
Ransomware		The redirection from a user's website to a fraudulent site, by modifying their DNS entries.
Trojan		Limits or denies a user access to their system until a ransom is paid.

4 Describe how a phishing scam might allow a cyber criminal to gain someone's bank details via telephone. **[3]**

....

....

....

System Security and Software

5 A controversial pop star has had their website closed by a DoS attack, and has been told that they need to pay a ransom to release the website.

Describe how this happened. **[3]**

_____

_____

_____

6 A network policy informs members of an organization about what they are and are not allowed to do when they are using on-site computers.

State **three** aspects of a user's work life that might be covered by this policy. **[3]**

_____

_____

_____

Threat Prevention

1 Describe **three** ways in which encryption can improve the security of an organization's network. **[3]**

_____

_____

_____

2 Why must anti-malware be updated regularly? **[2]**

_____

_____

3 An organization that is concerned with its online security access hires an expert in penetration testing to try to access its system.

What will the expert be looking for during the penetration testing? [3]

....

....

....

4 Describe the difference between a public encryption key and a private encryption key. [2]

....

....

5 A social network would like users to improve their security settings, and it wants to provide a list of five top tips for creating a strong password.

State **five** pieces of advice the social network might offer in its list. [5]

....

....

....

....

6 A hospital has been advised to set user access levels for the staff who use its computer network.

State **three** possible reasons for this advice. [3]

....

....

....

System Security and Software

1 Describe **two** user benefits of a modern GUI. [2]

2 Match each term with its definition. [4]

Third-party applications	Software designed for work-related tasks, such as word processing.
Utility software	The software link between the hardware, software and user.
Operating system	Performs specific tasks, for example security, to support the operating system.
Application software	Designed by an external organization, often as an alternative software solution.

3 Describe **three** types of utility software. [3]

4 What is the difference between a full backup and an incremental backup? [2]

5 Why might the following types of organization need encryption software?

a) School [1]

b) Games designer [1]

c) Social network [1]

d) Hospital [1]

6 A small printing business has contacted a computer support consultant because their office machine is running slowly.

The consultant recommends using defragmentation utility software.

What is this and how does it work? [3]

Computer Networking

Wired and Wireless Networks 1

1 Describe what the abbreviations LAN and WAN stand for and the relationship between them. **[4]**

2 The Internet is described as the world's largest WAN, connecting LANs across the world. State **two** connection methods for information to travel between countries. **[2]**

3 Grace's Gadgets has a new office with a large LAN, but staff are puzzled as to why their network is so slow.

Describe **three** possible factors they should consider. **[3]**

4 Tariq has been using a peer-to-peer network for a while, but he is now concerned that some files are missing from his computer.

Why might this be the case? **[2]**

Computer Networking

5 Circle which of the following modern devices now include network connectivity. **[6]**

Toaster   LCD TV   Smartphone   Vacuum cleaner

    Internet radio   Games console   Tablet   Microwave

Media streamer   Amplifier   Desk lamp

6 Describe **two** advantages and **two** disadvantages of a client–server network. **[4]**

Wired and Wireless Networks 2

1 Describe the difference between a switch and a router. **[2]**

2 Put the following transmission methods in order of potential distance of data travelled, with the shortest first. **[3]**

Fibre optic, Ethernet, Wi-Fi

3 If the Internet we know and use today is a vast interconnected collection of networks, then what is the World Wide Web? **[2]**

4 Describe **three** ways in which cloud computing would be beneficial to a travel reporter. **[3]**

5 Using cloud technology, the travel reporter does find **one** problem while working away from home. What is it? **[1]**

6 What is DNS and how does it help users browse the internet? **[2]**

Network Topologies

1 Draw diagrams to represent a star network topology and a mesh network topology. **[2]**

2 A nursery school wants to create a small network but cannot decide between a star and a mesh topology.

Provide **one** key advantage and **one** key disadvantage of each topology. **[4]**

Computer Networking

3 Name **two** other types of network topology. [2]

_____

_____

4 What device, which is part of all network topologies, will cause the network to fail if it is damaged, and why? [2]

_____

_____

5 Describe a potential problem of a ring network. [2]

_____

_____

6 Why does a mesh network require more cabling than other topologies? [1]

_____

Protocols and Layers

1 Wi-Fi broadcast signals are divided into channels. What benefit do these channels offer? [2]

_____

_____

2 While visiting a fast-food restaurant, Jack receives a smartphone notification warning him about connecting to an open unsecure network.

Why should he be concerned? [3]

_____

_____

_____

Computer Networking

3 What should Jack look for when connecting to Wi-Fi networks? **[2]**

4 An elderly couple and a mobile florist business have both set up their first email accounts. Which email protocol might be the most appropriate for each, and why? **[4]**

5 Which layer is primarily concerned with the communication of IP addresses between network routers? **[1]**

6 Describe the process of packet switching and state **three** key elements that each packet contains. **[4]**

Ethical, Legal, Cultural and Environmental Concerns

Ethical and Legal Concerns

1 A government employee loses his smartphone. He needs to retrieve it because he is concerned about its contents.

Describe **three** systems that could be used to try to locate it. [3]

_____

_____

_____

2 Judy joins a large social network and is surprised to find that all of the services it offers are free.

Explain how large social networks generate income. [4]

_____

_____

_____

_____

3 Governments around the world would like to monitor our digital footprint so that they can identify potentially dangerous threats.

Provide **three** examples of what the term 'digital footprint' refers to. [3]

_____

_____

_____

4 Describe **three** examples of situations where automated devices can work in locations potentially dangerous to humans. [3]

_____

_____

_____

Ethical, Legal, Cultural and Environmental Concerns

5 Describe how criminals are using the Internet to commit offences in the following areas.

   a) Films and TV   **[1]**

   b) Banking   **[1]**

   c) Motor vehicles   **[1]**

   d) Illegal substances   **[1]**

6 Ray is in his first term at university. He receives a letter saying that he and his housemates have been breaking copyright laws and their Internet connection is to be taken down. He does not understand why this has happened.
State **two** possible reasons why this has happened.   **[2]**

Cultural and Environmental Concerns

1 State an example of how computer technology might affect the life of a typical adult in each of the following situations.

   a) Accessing the local and international news at breakfast time.   **[1]**

   b) Listening to music on the train to work.   **[1]**

   c) Working as an estate agent.   **[1]**

d) Booking a holiday over lunch.   [1]

....

e) Talking to family during the evening.   [1]

....

f) Evening meal time.   [1]

....

g) Watching a movie.   [1]

....

h) Reading.   [1]

....

2 Explain how online tutorials and videos have changed the ways in which children and adults can learn new skills.   [4]

....

....

....

....

3 Briefly describe the term 'digital divide'.   [2]

....

....

Ethical, Legal, Cultural and Environmental Concerns

4 Complete the following table on the positive and negatives impacts of technology on the environment. Add a tick in the 'positive' or 'negative' column for each, as appropriate. **[10]**

	Positive	Negative
Increased energy consumption of digital devices.		
Increased greenhouse gas emissions to meet additional power needs.		
Reductions in the amount of paper used.		
Devices often include toxic materials.		
The design of increasingly efficient renewable energy production.		
It is difficult to recycle waste materials from outdated or unwanted technology.		
Downloads instead of physical media reduce material costs.		
The transportation and use of raw and synthetic materials in the production of smart devices.		
Mobile and home working reduces transportation costs.		
Smarter devices control their energy usage to meet our needs – this reduces wastage.		

5 Briefly describe why the number of unwanted electrical devices is increasing faster than ever before. **[2]**

....

....

6 How might technology one day help a surgeon to perform an operation from a remote location? **[2]**

....

....

Ethical, Legal, Cultural and Environmental Concerns

Computer Science Legislation

1 State **four** principles of the Data Protection Act 1998. [4]

....

....

....

....

2 What is meant by the term 'copyright'? [2]

....

....

....

3 Paul is a designer who wants to add high-quality photos to his promotional website.

State **three** legal ways he might achieve this. [3]

....

....

....

Ethical, Legal, Cultural and Environmental Concerns

4 Match each piece of legislation with its definition. **[5]**

Data Protection Act 1998	To prevent the hacking and damaging of computer systems.
Computer Misuse Act 1990	To provide creators of media with the right to control how their products are accessed and sold.
Copyright, Designs and Patents Act 1988	To provide the public with a right to information held by central and local government.
Creative Commons Licensing	To protect the personal information held about individuals within organizations.
Freedom of Information Act 2000	To provide licences that allow people to use, share and edit pieces of work.

5 Many e-books are now listed as in the public domain.

Explain what this means. **[2]**

....

....

6 Fiona is opening a cupcake business and has been advised to use open source software to save money.

What does the term 'open source' mean? **[2]**

....

....

Algorithms and Computational Logic

Algorithms and Flow Diagrams

1. An amusement park ride program opens and closes an entry gate until the maximum number of people have got on the ride. What type of algorithm is this? **[1]**

2. A programmer has been asked to create a virtual driving simulator. How will abstraction help him to design a solution? **[2]**

3. Why must a data set be ordered when a binary search is carried out? **[3]**

4. Carry out a bubble sort on the data set (6,2,4,1,8) to put the values in ascending order. **[5]**

5. A linear search is sometimes referred to as a 'brute force' search. Why is this? **[2]**

Algorithms and Computational Logic

6 Draw the correct flow chart shape for the following functions: **[5]**

Start/stop	
Input/output	
Decision	
Process	
Sub-program/sub-routine	

Pseudocode 1

1 What is the difference between pseudocode and a programming language such as Python? **[2]**

2 State **two** pseudocode keywords that might be used in a program to provide a response **a)** if a statement is met and **b)** if a statement is not met. **[2]**

3 Explain the term 'naming convention' and provide **two** defined coding examples. [4]

4 Within a program, what is the difference between a variable and a constant? [2]

5 A music streaming algorithm is being written by a team of developers. Why is the use of comments so important? [2]

6 Write a simple program that is used to check the weight of luggage being put into the hold of a plane. If the value is greater than 30, then 'Too heavy' is displayed; otherwise, 'OK' is displayed. [4]

Algorithms and Computational Logic

Pseudocode 2

1 What does the following pseudocode do? [3]

```
t = 0
while t <= 50
      print t
      t = t + 1
endwhile
```

....

....

....

2 Describe the difference between the operators MOD and DIV. [2]

....

....

3 Write a simple program that asks for the three dimensions required and then calculates and returns the volume of a room. [5]

Algorithms and Computational Logic

4. Describe the purpose of the following short program. [3]

```
stepOne = input("Please enter your password")
stepTwo = input("Please confirm your password again")
if stepOne == stepTwo then
    print("Access granted")
else
    print("Access denied")
end
```

5. What common element do a variable and a constant share? [1]

6. Write a short program that allows cheaper train tickets to be bought for children under 16 OR adults over 65. A cheap ticket costs £10; a standard ticket costs £20. [3]

Computational Logic

1. Draw the standard shapes for an AND, OR and NOT gate. [3]

2 Create a truth table for the following logic circuit. **[5]**

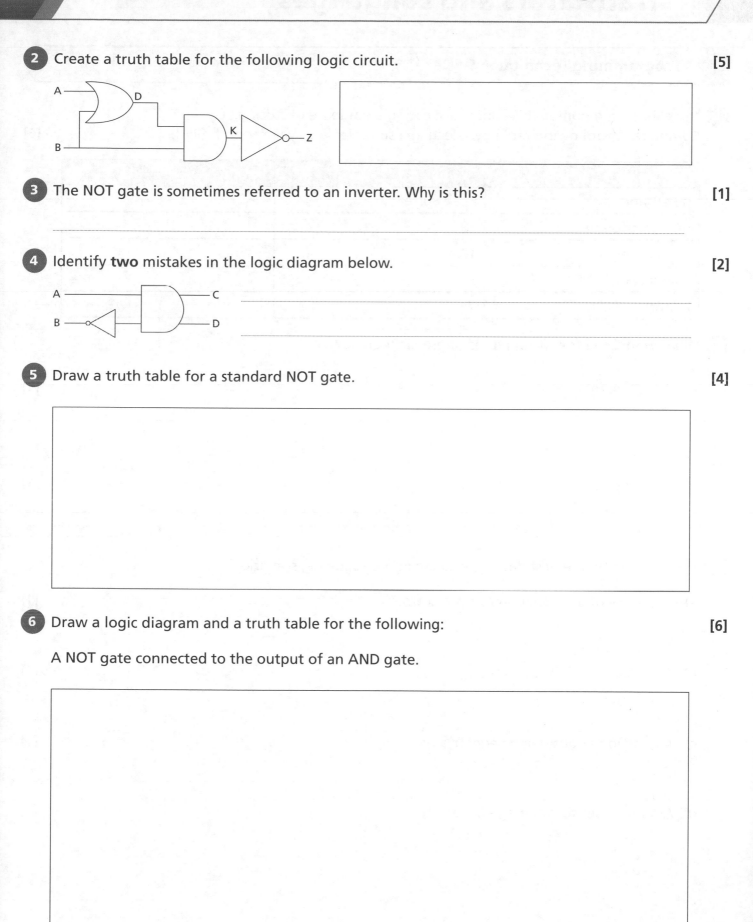

3 The NOT gate is sometimes referred to an inverter. Why is this? **[1]**

....

4 Identify **two** mistakes in the logic diagram below. **[2]**

....

....

5 Draw a truth table for a standard NOT gate. **[4]**

6 Draw a logic diagram and a truth table for the following: **[6]**

A NOT gate connected to the output of an AND gate.

Programming Techniques, Programs, Translators and Languages

Programming Techniques 1

1 Nik's Shack, a mountain bike shop, is creating a database of stock bikes. Complete the following table by selecting a suitable data type for each field. **[5]**

Field	Example	Data type
bikeBrand	Peak Buster	
numberofGears	18	
overallWeight	10.4	
colourCode	S	
inStock	Yes	

2 What would the following pieces of pseudocode do?

a) `int("1977")` **[1]**

b) `str(3827)` **[1]**

3 What would be the best data type to use in the following scenarios?

a) The entry of an alphanumeric password. **[1]**

b) The precise weight of a metal. **[1]**

c) A question about being vegetarian. **[1]**

d) Asking a user for their age in years. **[1]**

Programming Techniques, Programs, Translators and Languages

4 Explain the term 'concatenation' in relation to programming. [2]

....

....

5 Write a simple program that does the following: [4]

a) asks for the first and last name of the user

b) asks for the year of birth of the user

c) takes the first letter of the first name, the first letter of the last name and the year of birth to generate a username, and returns this on screen.

....

....

....

....

6 Consider a text file called 'story.txt'. Write a short program to open the file and print the first line. [4]

....

....

....

....

Programming Techniques, Programs, Translators and Languages

Programming Techniques 2

1 Nik's Shack now has a database of mountain bikes in stock, which is called 'Stock'.

bikeID	bikeBrand	numberofGears	overallWeight	colourCode	inStock
0001	Peak Buster	18	10.4	S	Yes
0002	PB Wheelers	21	13.2	R	Yes
0003	Peak Buster	24	11.3	G	No
0004	Team PB	18	12.4	B	Yes
0005	PB Wheelers	24	14.3	Y	Yes

a) How many records does the database have? [1]

b) How many fields does each record have? [1]

c) What would be the problem with a single character colour code? [1]

d) Which field is the primary key? [1]

2 Still looking at Nik's Shack 'Stock' database, write SQL statements to carry out the following tasks.

a) Create the database fields. [1]

b) Search for all bikes that have more than 20 gears. [1]

c) Search for bikes that have 18 gears AND are in stock. [1]

Programming Techniques, Programs, Translators and Languages

3 a) Write a short program to create a one-dimensional array of the race lap times shown. **[2]**

	0	1	2	3
Laptime	59.4	64.3	74.3	81.9

b) How might this be turned into a two-dimensional array? **[1]**

4 State **three** reasons why a programmer will use sub-routines to improve a program. **[3]**

5 Sub-routines can contain both parameters and arguments.
Describe the difference between these. **[2]**

6 Oscar is writing a weather application and will be using multiple sub-routines.

a) Write a short sub-routine to carry out a conversion from Celsius to Fahrenheit when required. **[4]**

Note: F = (C × 1.8) + 32

b) Why is Oscar using a function rather than a procedure? **[1]**

Programming Techniques, Programs, Translators and Languages

Producing Robust Programs

1 Daisy is writing a program to be used in a school classroom. A friend has reminded her to consider defensive design when designing a system to be used by children.

   a) What is defensive design? **[2]**

   b) Describe **three** ways in which this can be applied to a system to be used by children. **[3]**

2 Andrew is just starting out as a programmer and a colleague provides him with a list of tips to keep his programs well maintained.
Describe **four** tips for good program maintenance. **[4]**

3 When checking through a first version of an address book program, Rachel finds several syntax and logic errors.
What are the differences between these two types of error? **[2]**

4 Logic errors are often more difficult to solve. Why might this be the case? **[2]**

Programming Techniques, Programs, Translators and Languages

5 Testing is an essential part of the design process. Match each term with its definition. **[6]**

Iterative testing	Carried out by real users to find issues not considered by the original designer.
Final testing	Will the program crash if several users access it at once?
Performance testing	An examination of how user-friendly the system is.
Usability testing	How vulnerable is the program to attacks, and is the data secure?
Security testing	The impact the program will have on system resources when it is run.
Load/stress testing	A cycle of design, development and testing, with the results of testing fed back into the loop.

6 Pawel is carrying out tests on a computer-based version of a popular board game. Why is it important to create and test extreme and erroneous data as well as normal data? **[2]**

....

....

Translators and Facilities of Languages

1 Isaac has been asked to choose a high-level programming language to focus on during a university course.
Investigate and note down at least **four** current languages open to him. **[4]**

....

....

....

Programming Techniques, Programs, Translators and Languages

2 Having chosen a high-level programming language and written his first program, Isaac must now convert his work to machine code using a translator.
Identify **two** types of translator that can achieve this and the process involved. **[4]**

3 Many programmers still specialize in using low-level languages. State **two** reasons why this might be the case. **[2]**

4 Noah has written a financial application using an integrated development environment, and the code editor function has helped him to identify syntax errors.
Describe **two** ways this might have happened. **[2]**

5 Match each IDE functionality with its description. **[4]**

Code editors	This will compile or interpret the final code as required.
Error diagnostics	This allows programs to be run virtually within the IDE software.
Run-time environment	Also known as debugging tools, these will help to identify errors in particular lines of code.
Translators	These are designed for writing source code, with tools to assist with formatting and syntax.

6 State **three** ways in which an IDE helps a programmer to spot and rectify logic errors. **[3]**

Data Representation

Units and Formats of Data

1 Match each typical file type with its associated unit of data. **[4]**

high-definition video		terabytes
MP3 audio file		kilobytes
system backup files		megabytes
word processing document		gigabytes

2 Why does the extended ASCII character set have 256 characters, rather than the 128 characters of the original ASCII set? **[2]**

3 What is the name of the character set designed as a world industry standard? **[1]**

4 What are the ASCII numbers of the following characters?

   a) The UK pound symbol. **[1]**

   b) The division symbol. **[1]**

   c) An upper-case K. **[1]**

   d) An exclamation mark. **[1]**

5 Why was an extra zero added to the original version of 7-bit ASCII? **[1]**

Data Representation

6 State **three** non-printed commands that can be represented by a character set such as extended ASCII. [3]

_____

_____

_____

Converting Data 1

1 Convert the following denary numbers into binary.

a) 18 [1]

_____

b) 25 [1]

_____

c) 251 [1]

_____

d) 161 [1]

_____

2 Add the following binary numbers and then convert the answer into denary.

a) 00000101 + 11100101 [2]

_____

_____

b) 00110101 + 00100100 [2]

_____

_____

Data Representation

3 Write a binary addition calculation that will result in a binary overflow. [1]

4 Carry out a left shift of 1 on the following binary numbers.

a) 00110101 [1]

b) 00100110 [1]

5 Carry out a right shift of 1 on the following binary numbers.

a) 11010100 [1]

b) 01011010 [1]

6 What is the practical purpose of using left and right shifts with binary numbers? [1]

Converting Data 2

1 Convert the following denary numbers into hexadecimal.

a) 254 [1]

b) 99 [1]

c) 42 [1]

Data Representation

2. Using the ASCII table, the phrase BIG can be represented in binary as:

01000010   01001001   01000111

Convert this binary sequence into a hexadecimal number sequence.   [3]

3. Convert the following hexadecimal numbers into denary.

   a) 4F   [1]

   b) 8C   [1]

   c) 12   [1]

4. Why might a programmer claim that hexadecimal is easier to work with than binary? [1]

5. What mistake might a new programmer make when working with the hexadecimal
   number 24?   [1]

6. A website offering secure shopping needs to make sure that the credit card numbers its users
   enter are genuine.

   What system will it use and how does the system work?   [2]

Data Representation

1 How many bits would be needed to create an image with:

   a) 2 colours?   **[1]**

   b) 4 colours?   **[1]**

   c) 16 colours?   **[1]**

2 State **two** ways in which a photo management program will use metadata.   **[2]**

3 Describe the benefit and the drawback of sampling an analogue audio recording at a very high bit-rate.   **[2]**

4 Why is the RAW image format popular with professional photographers?   **[1]**

5 Why might using JPEG files cause a problem for a designer who regularly edits the same images more than once?   **[2]**

6 Audio podcasts are very popular with users of smartphones.
What file type is normally used, and why?   **[2]**

Collins

GCSE Computer Science
Paper 1: Computer Systems

Time allowed: 1 hour 30 minutes

Instructions

- Use black ink.
- Answer **all** the questions.
- Write your answer to each question in the spaces provided.
- You may **not** use a calculator.

Information

- The total mark for this paper is **80**.
- The marks for questions are shown in brackets **[ ]**.
- Quality of extended responses will be assessed in this paper in questions marked with an *.

Name: _____

1 Elizabeth is a freelance journalist with her own blog. She posts articles, images and videos from all over the UK, but finds that her smartphone and digital camera quickly run out of storage space.

(a) One of the new cameras she is considering has an option to upload images to the 'cloud'. Explain what is meant by 'cloud storage'.

....

.... [1]

(b) Uploading files to the cloud brings advantages and disadvantages.

(i) Describe **two** advantages of storing files online.

....

.... [2]

(ii) Describe **two** disadvantages of storing files online.

....

.... [2]

(c) Elizabeth also considers using secondary storage devices for saving her files.

(i) Define the term 'secondary storage'.

....

.... [1]

(ii) Identify which storage technology would be the most appropriate for saving files on the move, and give a reason for your choice.

....

.... [2]

2 Joseph has a gaming PC he built himself. In recent months, after installing a new operating system, he finds that the PC has become slower and new games are not running well.

(a) State **two** reasons why operating systems are regularly updated.

_____

_____ [2]

(b) Joseph's friend recommends that he upgrade the RAM is his computer.

(i) Define the term 'RAM'.

_____

_____ [1]

(ii) Explain why having more RAM should allow a computer to run faster.

_____

_____ [2]

(c) Having done some research, Joseph decides to try to reconfigure his operating system before he upgrades the hardware. He experiments with virtual memory settings and disk defragmentation.

(i) Define the term 'virtual memory'.

_____

_____ [1]

(ii) State **one** advantage and **one** disadvantage of using virtual memory.

_____

_____ [2]

(iii) Explain the process of disk defragmentation.

_____

_____ [2]

3   A cycle-hire business, specializing in electric bikes, has expanded to a second shop in a woodland area. The business makes use of computers and tablet devices for bookings, and they need to make sure that they have a reliable system in place.

(a) Devices in the shop are connected to a LAN.

   (i) Define the term 'LAN'.

   _____

   _____ [1]

   (ii) State how the business owners could connect the LAN in their second shop to the LAN in their original shop, and state the device needed to connect them together.

   _____

   _____ [2]

(b) Wireless technology is used in the shop and the owners are concerned about its security.

   (i) State **three** wireless encryption standards that they could consider.

   _____

   _____

   _____ [3]

   (ii) Explain which standard they should use and why.

   _____

   _____ [2]

(c) The shop also has a children's seating area with tablet computers for children to play cycle games and look at videos while parents make bookings. These devices run on a virtual network.

   (i) Define the term 'virtual network'.

   _____

   _____ [1]

(ii) Explain why these tablet computers were set up in this way.

_____

_____ **[1]**

4   An independent film production company specializes in creating film shorts on a budget that still look like slick Hollywood productions. All of their films are shot and edited digitally, and the company is constantly looking for new software and media clips it can use.

(a) State which legislative Act applies to the following aspects of their business.

   (i) Concerns about their films being pirated and shared online before official release.

_____ **[1]**

   (ii) Making sure the personal details of all employees and customers are secure.

_____ **[1]**

   (iii) Using music and stock footage available online in their films.

_____ **[1]**

(b) When editing film and music tracks, the company can save their files in either lossy or lossless format.

   (i) Explain the difference between the two formats.

_____

_____

_____ **[2]**

   (ii) State which format would be the more appropriate when editing content and explain why this would be the case.

_____

_____ **[2]**

(c) Live bands are often brought in to the editing studio to create a high-quality original recording. Explain the process of transferring their analogue recording to a digital format.

....

....

....

.... **[3]**

5   David runs a small network consultant business. He works with larger organizations to stop potential computer problems before they happen and to test their networks for weaknesses.

(a) Two of the services David offers are penetration testing and network forensics.

(i) Define the term 'penetration testing'.

....

.... **[1]**

(ii) Define the term 'network forensics'.

....

.... **[1]**

(b) Many of the organizations he works with dispose of unwanted, but still serviceable, equipment straight to landfill.

(i) State **three** reasons for not doing this.

....

....

.... **[3]**

(ii) State an ethical alternative to disposing of unwanted equipment.

....

.... **[1]**

6   A world news organization is expanding its website to include a subscription service that will pay for additional journalists around the world. The organization is very concerned with security, as an older version of its website was often attacked.

(a) The original website was the victim of a DoS attack. Define the term 'DoS attack'.

....

.... [1]

(b) Subscription customers are reminded to create a strong password when setting up their account.

(i) State **three** pieces of password advice.

....

....

....

.... [3]

(ii) Explain how hackers are often able to guess or calculate a password.

....

.... [2]

(c) The subscription page of the site is a HTTPS page.

(i) Define the term 'HTTPS'.

....

.... [1]

(ii) HTTPS is a network protocol. Explain what is meant by a network protocol.

....

.... [1]

(d) Customers of the original website were often targeted by malware. State **three** different pieces of malware and explain the damage each can cause.

_____

_____

_____

_____

_____

_____

_____

_____

_____

_____ **[6]**

7   Mateusz wants to set up a new computer science classroom using a client–server system. It is important that the server is powerful enough to serve multiple workstations. He has narrowed it down to three choices; see **Fig. 1.**

Fig. 1

Server 1	Server 2	Server 3
CPU Clock Speed: 2.4 GHz	CPU Clock Speed: 1.8 GHz	CPU Clock Speed: 2 GHz
CPU Cores: 2	CPU Cores: 1	CPU Cores: 4
Hard Drive Space: 500 GB	Hard Drive Space: 750 GB	Hard Drive Space: 1 TB

(a) State which is the most appropriate server and identify **two** reasons for this.

[3]

(b) A star network topology has been chosen. Describe **two** advantages and **two** disadvantages of using this network type.

[4]

(c) Explain **three** benefits a network manager will get from using client workstations in the classroom.

[3]

8   A university is adding an encryption algorithm to its campus messaging system because students are concerned about their messages being intercepted.

(a) Define the term 'encryption'.

[1]

(b) The system is designed to encrypt data packets. Describe the process of how data packets travel from one location to another.

....

....

....

....

[3]

9*   An international bank has set up new network systems across the world, with a key focus on the user access level of its employees.

Discuss the reasons for setting appropriate user access levels for large network users. In your answer, you might consider the following:

- Security
- Employee responsibilities
- Fraud
- Legislation.

....

....

....

....

....

....

....

....

....

....

....

[8]

GCSE Computer Science

Paper 2: Computational Thinking, Algorithms and Programming

Time allowed: 1 hour 30 minutes

Instructions

- Use black ink.
- Answer **all** the questions.
- Write your answer to each question in the spaces provided.
- You may **not** use a calculator.

Information

- The total mark for this paper is **80**.
- The marks for questions are shown in brackets **[ ]**.

Name: _____

1 **(a)** Add the missing unit from the following ordered list.

MB   GB   __   PB

.... **[1]**

(b) Convert the decimal number 249 into an 8-bit binary number.

.... **[1]**

(c) Trying to convert the number 259 into an 8 bit binary number results in an overflow. Define the term 'overflow'.

.... **[1]**

(d) Add the following binary numbers together and give the answer as a binary and a decimal number:

10010010

00001100

....

.... **[2]**

(e) Convert the hexadecimal number E9 into a decimal number and show your working.

....

.... **[2]**

(f) A UK mobile telephone number in the format 07######## will often need to be written in the international format +447########.

(i) Write an algorithm that asks for a UK mobile number, replaces the first 0 with the prefix +44 and returns the result to the user. It should also return 'not recognised' for numbers not starting with a '0'.

[5]

(ii) The international UK number begins with the + symbol. State the most suitable data type for handling this symbol.

[1]

2   Fiona has a database of customers at her garage. The database is called VipCustomers; see **Fig. 1.**

Fig. 1.

custID	surname	firstName	carsBought	houseNumber	postCode	contactNumber
0001	Beck	Charlotte	3	161	VC1 4RD	07123827645
0002	Dawson	Philip	2	9	VC2 7YT	01293837645
0003	DeSouza	Peter	4	32	VC7 3EK	01293695641
0004	Parker	Kate	1	4	VC2 4RD	07256453726

(a) Describe the difference between a record and a field.

_____

_____ **[2]**

(b) Create database searches using Structured Query Language (SQL) to display the following.

(i) All the records of customers who have bought only one car.

_____ **[1]**

(ii) The first name of customers who have bought three or more cars.

_____ **[1]**

(iii) The first name, surname and contact number of customers from the VC2 4RD postcode.

_____ **[1]**

3   Consider the following data sequence: 13, 32, 10, 19.

(a) Show the stages of a bubble sort when applied to this sequence.

....

....

....

....

....

....   [3]

(b) Describe the process of carrying out a linear search on the same sequence to find the value 10.

....

....

....

....

....   [3]

(c) A linear search is inefficient for large datasets. State the type of search that should be used for these.

....   [1]

4   Ivan manages an ice hockey team and is building a program to record the goals scored. **Fig. 2**, titled goalsScored, shows the names of three players and the number of goals they have scored.

Fig. 2

	0	1	2	3
0	Wayne	3	3	2
1	Mario	2	4	5
2	Bobby	6	4	7

(a) It has been recommended that Ivan should use an array.

   (i) Write an algorithm to create this table as a two-dimensional array.

   [3]

   (ii) Write a short search algorithm to return the number of goals scored by Mario in his third game.

   [1]

(b) In respect to the amount of data it can store, state how a one-dimensional array differs from a two-dimensional array.

   [1]

5 Amelia is writing a program (see **Fig. 3**) that simulates two dice being rolled to start a board game. The numbers on both dice need to match for the game to start. If not, they are rolled again.

Fig. 3

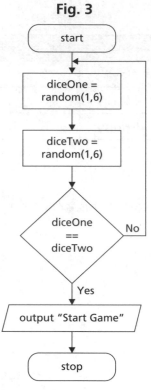

(a) State **two** variables in the program.

....

.... [2]

(b) Explain the process taking place within the diamond shape.

....

....

.... [2]

(c) It has been suggested that this program could form a sub-routine used in a variety of games.

   (i) Define the term 'sub-routine'.

....

.... [1]

(ii) Write a short program representing the flow chart as a sub-routine.

[3]

(iii) Describe whether this sub-routine would be a function or a procedure.

[1]

(d) The final program will be written using an integrated development environment (IDE) to translate the high-level programming language into machine code.

(i) Define the term 'high-level programming language'.

[1]

(ii) State the **three** translator options open to programmers and briefly define the purpose of each.

[6]

6   Consider a two-level logic circuit with three inputs, A, B and C, and an output X.

   (a) Create a logic circuit diagram that represents the Boolean expression:

   (i) X = (A OR B) AND (NOT C).

   ....

   ....

   ....

   ....

   ....

   ....

   ....

   ....   **[3]**

   (ii) Complete the following truth table for the same expression.

A	B	C	X

                                                                                                  [8]

(b) Describe the purpose of the following logic circuit.

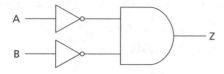

....

....

.... **[2]**

7   Cathy has written a program to convert Celsius into Fahrenheit. Users are asked to enter a temperature in Celsius; a calculation is carried out and the value is returned to them in Fahrenheit.

```
tempC = input("Please enter the temperature in Celsius")
tempF = tempC * 1.8 + 32
print (tempF)
```

(a) Before writing her program, Cathy broke the task down into smaller tasks and then removed all unnecessary information to provide focus. State the **two** computational thinking skills she used.

....

.... **[2]**

(b) Define how Cathy could leave guidance for others adapting her code later.

....

.... **[1]**

(c) The program is being adapted to also provide a response to the user about whether the current temperature in Fahrenheit is above or below the average temperature. The average is represented by the variable 'averageTemp'. Improve the original program to include this functionality.

[4]

(d) Cathy always runs careful tests before releasing any program. State the **three** types of data she would use to test her calculations and briefly define their purpose.

[6]

8   Noah is part of a development team that writes smartphone applications. He specialises in the graphical and audio elements. A graphical icon has the hexadecimal code: 69 96

(a) Convert the hexadecimal code into a series of binary numbers and complete the table below to show the icon. Use 0 = White and 1 = Black.

[5]

(b) The application is limited to a 4-bit image. State how many colours this would allow.

.... [1]

(c) JPEG compression is used to save all images used in the application. Define **one** advantage and **one** disadvantage of this file format.

....

....

....

....

.... [2]

Notes

Answers

The Purpose and Function of the Central Processing Unit

1.

Input	A device that sends information or data to the CPU.
Output	A device that receives instructions or data from the CPU.
Software	Programmed instructions for a computer with a specific task.
Hardware	Any physical device that would normally form part of a computer system.

[4]

2.

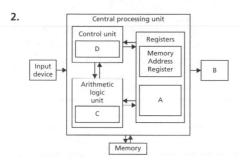

[4]

3. Bus [1]
4. The arithmetic logic unit (ALU) is where calculations are carried out, and the results of these calculations are stored in the accumulator until they are needed [2]
5. The control unit [1]
6. Stored program means that both the computer program and the data it processes are stored in memory [2]

Systems Architecture

1. Clock speed is the rate at which instructions are processed by the CPU [1]
2. Multi-core processors have more than one CPU on the same chip [1]; this means that tasks can be carried out simultaneously, which speeds up the system [1]
3. The L1 cache is used to store very frequently accessed data; it is quite small but very fast [1]. The L2 cache is slower and further away, but it is still more efficient that main memory [1]
4. The whole system may still function if a non-essential embedded system is damaged [1]. Different manufacturers can simultaneously work on embedded systems during production [1]
5. Any **four** of the following:
   An instruction is fetched from memory [1]
   The instruction is then decoded [1]
   The decoded instruction is then executed so that the CPU performs continuously [1]
   The process is repeated [1]
   The program counter is incremented [1]
   The instruction is transferred to the MDR [1]
   The address of the instruction to be fetched is placed in the MAR [1]

6. Too many requests are being made of the CPU [1] and it cannot keep up, and so the system becomes slow and errors can occur [1]

Memory

1. RAM is a temporary area that a computer uses to store data in current use [1]
2. a) Volatile means that once power is switched off all data stored on is lost [1]. Non-volatile means that any instructions written are permanently kept without power [1]
   b) Manufacturers can write instructions to ROM, such as BIOS, and these cannot be changed or edited [1]
3. a) Basic input/output system [1]
   b) It ensures hardware communications [1]; it starts running the operating system [1]
4. a) It is created because the RAM becomes full [1]
   b) It is created on the hard drive [1]
   c) As hard drive communication is not as fast as RAM, the system will become slow if hard drive communication is used too much [1]
5. Unlike with RAM, the data stored will remain when power is disconnected [1]
6. Updates and new functionality can be added later because flash memory can be edited [1]

Storage Types, Devices and Characteristics

1. Any five of the following: capacity [1]; speed [1]; portability [1]; durability [1]; reliability [1]; cost [1]
2. a) CD [1]; DVD [1]; Blu-ray [1]
   b) Discs can be damaged easily [1]; capacity is limited by type [1]; the correct writer/player must be used [1]
3. The original device has more storage capacity [1], but the new device will run faster [1]
4. Any **two** of the following: An optical drive is slower to access than others [1], is liable to skip/jump if it is moved [1] and has limited capacity [1]
5. Magnetic storage is large [1] and has complex moving parts that could be damaged with physical use [1]
6. At regular intervals, move the stored files to a new storage media technology [1]

Common System Threats

1. Any four of the following: usernames [1]; passwords [1]; bank account numbers [1]; personal email addresses [1]; answers to secret questions [1]; full names [1]
2. A virus must be transferred from one computer to another via another file [1], for example an email attachment, whereas a worm can replicate itself between systems [1]
3.

Pharming	The redirection from a user's website to a fraudulent site, by modifying their DNS entries.
Ransomware	Limits or denies a user access to their system until a ransom is paid.
Trojan	Installed by a user who thinks it is a legitimate piece of software when it is, in fact, malware.

[3]

4. Telephone a member of the public, pretending to be their bank [1], ask them to confirm and obtain their bank details following a fictitious security problem [1], and then use these to commit a crime [1]
5. The website was flooded with false data traffic [1], causing the server to crash [1], and this will be repeated until a ransom is paid [1]
6. The transfer of files to and from the workplace [1]; Internet browsing rules [1]; the use of personal devices in the workplace [1]

Threat Prevention
1. Encrypted files can be stored safely [1], with no external access from unwanted users [1], and messages intercepted between organization staff cannot be read [1]
2. As new virus codes appear every day [1], anti-malware software must be updated to include the latest patches [1]
3. Any three of the following: weak passwords [1]; previously unknown access methods [1]; system areas vulnerable to virus attack [1]; potential SQL injection areas [1]
4. A public key is known by all and is a method used to encrypt a message [1], but the private key needed to decrypt the message is known only to the recipient of the message [1]
5. Any five of the following: make sure they are at least eight characters long [1]; use upper- and lower-case characters [1], include special characters [1]; avoid real dictionary words [1]; avoid any personal information [1]; regularly change any password [1]
6. Ensuring that staff cannot access personal information [1]; making sure that any sensitive data cannot be removed from the network [1]; making sure that external devices, which potentially carry viruses, cannot be used [1]

System Software
1. Users do not have to use command prompt text functions [1] and users can visually drag and drop files [1]
2.

Third-party applications	Designed by an external organization, often as an alternative software solution.
Utility software	Performs specific tasks, for example security, to support the operating system.
Operating system	The software link between the hardware, software and user.
Application software	Software designed for work-related tasks, such as word processing.

[4]

3. Any three of the following: firewalls [1]; anti-malware [1]; encryption services [1]; defragmentation [1]; compression [1]; backup software [1]
4. A full backup copies all important files to an external source [1]; an incremental backup will copy only the files that have changed since the previous backup [1]
5. a) To keep students' personal details private [1]
   b) To protect unreleased games from being accessed and stolen [1]
   c) To keep the usernames and passwords secure [1]
   d) To protect the medical records of patients [1]

6. Defragmentation utility software analyses data and how it is stored on a disk [1]. It then rearranges files into a more logical sequence [1] to allow faster access [1]

Pages 159–163 **Computer Networking**

Wired and Wireless Networks 1
1. Local area network (LAN) [1]; wide area network (WAN) [1]. A WAN is formed by connecting one or more LAN together [1] across large distances [1]
2. Fibre-optic cables [1]; satellites [1]
3. Network bandwidth [1]; interference from external factors and devices [1]; the number of users connecting at the same time [1]
4. He may have not checked the permission settings of the network [1] and so other users have been allowed access to his files [1]
5. LCD TV [1]; smartphone [1]; Internet radio [1]; games console [1]; tablet [1]; media streamer [1]
6. Advantages: software and security settings are controlled centrally [1]; client computers can be of relatively low specification [1]. Disadvantages: if the server fails, so does the network [1]; low-specification client machines can run quite slowly [1]

Wired and Wireless Networks 2
1. A switch connects network compatible devices together on the same network [1], whereas a router connects different networks together [1]
2. Shortest first: Wi-Fi, Ethernet, fibre optic [3]
3. A system to publish linked pages written in HTML [1] that can be viewed using a web browser anywhere in the world [1]
4. Files can be saved and accessed anywhere [1]; word processing and image editing software can be accessed via a browser [1]; storage devices do not need to be carried [1]
5. Without an Internet connection, cloud services cannot be accessed [1]
6. Domain Name Server or Service [1] is an Internet naming service that links the IP address of a computer on a network to a text-based website address that is easier to remember [1]

Network Topologies
1.

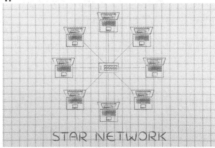

STAR NETWORK

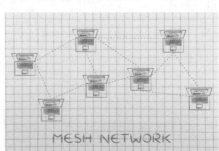

MESH NETWORK

[2]

2. Any of the following:
   Star advantages: the failure of a device, as long as it is not the server, will not halt the network [1]; the network can be expanded by adding devices [1]; localized problems can

be identified quickly [1]; data can be directed to a specific address via the central server [1]
Star disadvantages: if the server fails, the whole network will collapse [1]; extensive cabling and technical knowledge is needed to maintain the server [1]
Mesh advantages: all devices share the network load [1]; if a device fails, the network will continue to run [1]; adding more devices will not affect the speed of the network [1]
Mesh disadvantages: managing the network requires a high level of network expertise [1]; it can be expensive to set up because of the number of devices required [1]
3. Bus [1] and ring [1]
4. The server [1]. It directs the flow of data between devices [1]
5. Because the data travels in one direction, any device failure [1] will cause the network to fail [1]
6. Every device in the network needs to be connected to every other device in the network [1]

Protocols and Layers

1. Using channels with slightly different frequencies means that devices can run on the same network [1] without interference and signal loss [1]
2. An open unsecure network can be connected to by any device [1]; these devices may pass malware onto the network [1] and can potentially steal personal information [1]
3. An encrypted network connection [1] using WPA or WPA2 [1]
4. Elderly couple: Post Office Protocol [1], as all emails are downloaded to their home [1]. Florist: IMAP [1], as emails can be synced at home and on mobile devices on the move [1]
5. Internet (or Network) layer [1]
6. Data is broken down into packets, and routers direct data packets across multiple networks using the most efficient route [1]. Each packet contains the source and destination address [1], a portion of the data [1], and a reference to how the packets fits back together [1]

Pages 164–169 Ethical, Legal, Cultural and Environmental Concerns

Ethical and Legal Concerns

1. Triangulation using the mobile phone network [1]; GPS [1]; connection to Wi-Fi networks [1]
2. Organizations pay the social network to place advertising on the network [1]. Users' browsing habits on the network are tracked [1] and advertising is targeting at them [1] based on what they like and what their friends like [1]
3. Any three of the following: records of the websites we visit [1], the contents of instant messages/emails [1], the people we communicate with [1] and the locations of the devices we use [1]
4. Examples: scientific studies of a volcano [1]; bomb disposal [1]; deep underwater or space exploration [1]; nuclear or related power generation [1]
5. a) Sharing illegally obtained copies of new films/TV shows online [1]
   b) Stealing login details and transferring money to their own accounts [1]
   c) Selling cars through online auction sites without the proper paperwork [1]
   d) Selling drugs via online auction/dark websites without medical knowledge [1]
6. Any two of the following: using a peer-to-peer network to download films/TV shows [1]; downloading MP3s from an unofficial website [1]; sharing with friends links to websites illegally offering films/TV shows [1]

Cultural and Environmental Concerns

1. Examples:
   a) Watching news on a laptop via streaming site or listening to news via a smartphone radio app [1]
   b) Using a music streaming app/using wireless headphones [1]
   c) Placing advertisements around the world/receiving photos and text via email [1]

   d) Browsing destinations/watching video reviews/using comparison sites [1]
   e) Using video chat to talk to friends or relatives [1]
   f) Ordering a takeaway online or using an online recipe book [1]
   g) Downloading or streaming a film/booking cinema tickets online [1]
   h) Using an e-reader or reading a physical book that was ordered online [1]
2. Learning material can be accessed at any time [1] and in any place with an Internet connection [1]; material can be accessed that covers just about any topic [1] and it can be followed at the learners' own pace [1]
3. The digital divide is the social and economic gap [1] between those who have and those who do not have access to computer technology [1]
4.

	Positive	Negative
Increased energy consumption of digital devices.		✓
Increased greenhouse gas emissions to meet additional power needs.		✓
Reductions in the amount of paper used.	✓	
Devices often include toxic materials.		✓
The design of increasingly efficient renewable energy production.	✓	
It is difficult to recycle waste materials from outdated or unwanted technology.		✓
Downloads instead of physical media reduce material costs.	✓	
The transportation and use of raw and synthetic materials in the production of smart devices.		✓
Mobile and home working reduces transportation costs.	✓	
Smarter devices control their energy usage to meet our needs – this reduces wastage.	✓	

[10]

5. Users want the latest technology [1] before current technology comes to the end of its natural life [1]
6. Robotic/virtual technology could mimic the movements of the surgeon [1] across the Internet and recreate it at the patient's location [1]

Computer Science Legislation

1. Any four of the following:
   • Data should be fairly and lawfully processed [1]
   • Data must only be obtained and used for specified purposes [1]

- Data shall be adequate, relevant and not excessive **[1]**
- Data should be accurate and kept up to date **[1]**
- Data should not be kept for longer than necessary **[1]**
- Access must be granted to data subjects to check and correct their entries **[1]**
- Data must be kept safe and secure **[1]**
- Data should not be transferred outside the EEA to a country without adequate protection legislation **[1]**

2. Copyright is the legal right of the creators of music, books, films and games **[1]** to control how their products are accessed and sold **[1]**
3. Take the photos himself **[1]**; purchase royalty-free images online **[1]**; download photos from a website that provides free images for commercial use **[1]**
4.

Data Protection Act 1998	To protect the personal information held about individuals within organizations.
Computer Misuse Act 1990	To prevent the hacking and damaging of computer systems.
Copyright, Designs and Patents Act 1988	To provide creators of media with the right to control how their products are accessed and sold.
Creative Commons Licensing	To provide licences that allow people to use, share and edit pieces of work.
Freedom of Information Act 2000	To provide the public with a right to information held by central and local government.

[5]

5. The copyright and ownership of the book has expired **[1]**, meaning that the book can be used and shared for any purpose **[1]**
6. Open source software can be freely downloaded and shared online **[1]**, with no limitations on its use **[1]**

> Pages 170–175 **Algorithms and Computational Logic**

Algorithms and Flow Diagrams
1. Iteration **[1]**
2. Abstraction is the removal of unnecessary information **[1]**; focusing on the car and the road rather than on the surroundings will help to create a solution **[1]**
3. A binary search starts at the middle value **[1]**, then splits the data set **[1]** according to whether the data sought is above or below the middle value **[1]**
4. Five steps:
   (6,2,4,1,8) to (2,6,4,1,8) **[1]**
   (2,6,4,1,8) to (2,4,6,1,8) **[1]**
   (2,4,6,1,8) to (2,4,1,6,8) **[1]**
   (2,4,1,6,8) to (2,1,4,6,8) **[1]**
   (2,1,4,6,8) to (1,2,4,6,8) **[1]**
5. Because it goes through each of the items one by one, without prioritising them **[1]**, until it reaches the data sought **[1]**

6.

Start/stop		**[1]**
Input/output		**[1]**
Decision		**[1]**
Process		**[1]**
Sub-program/ sub-routine		**[1]**

Pseudocode 1
1. Pseudocode is not an official programming language designed to run on a computer **[1]**, so mistakes and plain English terms do not prevent it from being understood **[1]**
2. **a)** Else **[1]**; **b)** then **[1]**
3. A naming convention refers to the naming of variables with a simple rule **[1]** and keeping that rule applied throughout all similar programs **[1]**
   Examples: using two words to define a variable but removing the space and using a capital letter on the second **[1]**, for example engineSize or fuelTank **[1]**
4. The value attached to a variable can be changed within the same program **[1]**, but a constant cannot be changed because its value is fixed **[1]**
5. Without comments, it might be difficult for the developers to understand the reasons for each other's coding choices **[1]**; the developers can leave messages within the code to help each other **[1]**
6. Example:

```
Input weight                              [1]
If weight ≤ 30                            [1]
print 'OK' Else                           [1]
print 'Too heavy' End                     [1]
end
```

Pseudocode 2
1. Counts **[1]** and prints **[1]** numbers up to and including 50 **[1]**
2. MOD returns the remainder after a division **[1]**, while DIV divides but returns only a whole number (also known as an integer) **[1]**
3. Example:

```
length = input("what is the length of the room?")     [1]
width = input("what is the width of the room?")       [1]
height = input("what is the height of the room?")     [1]
volume = length * width * height                      [1]
print volume                                          [1]
end
```

4. A password is asked for twice **[1]**: if the two passwords match exactly **[1]** then access is granted, and if they do not match then access is not granted **[1]**
5. An identifier **[1]**
6. Example:

```
age = input("How old are you?")          [1]
if age < 16 OR age > 65 then
        price = 10                        [1]
else
        price = 20
print ("The ticket cost is: £" + price) [1]   [1]
end
```

Computational Logic

1. AND Gate

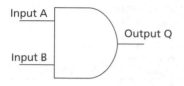

OR Gate

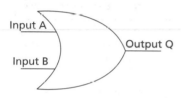

NOT Gate

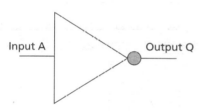

[3]

2.

A	B	D	K	Z	
0	0	0	0	1	**[1]**
0	1	1	1	0	**[1]**
1	0	1	0	1	**[1]**
1	1	1	1	0	**[1]**

3. The NOT gate inverts the signal, so a 0 input becomes a 1 output and vice versa **[1]**
4. The NOT gate is reversed **[1]** and the AND gate has two outputs instead of one **[1]**
5.

Inputs	Output
A	Q
0	1
1	0

[4]

6.

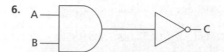

[2]

Inputs		Output
A	B	C
0	0	1
0	1	1
1	0	1
1	1	0

[4]

Pages 176–182 **Programming Techniques, Programs, Translators and Languages**

Programming Techniques 1

1.

Field	Example	Datatype
bikeBrand	Peak Buster	String
numberofGears	18	Integer
overallWeight	10.4	Real
colourCode	S	Character
inStock	Yes	Boolean

[5]

2. a) This converts the string 1977 to an integer **[1]**
   b) This converts the number 3827 to a string **[1]**
3. a) String **[1]**
   b) Real **[1]**
   c) Boolean **[1]**
   d) Integer **[1]**
4. Concatenation is the process of adding together two or more strings **[1]**, linking them together **[1]**
5. Example:

```
string1 = input("What is your first name?")        [1]
string2 = input("What is your last name?")
string3 = input("What year were you born?")
username = string1,[0] + string2,[0] + string3     [2]
    print(username)                                [1]
ond
```

6. Example:

```
myFile = openRead("story.txt")        [1]
lineOne = myFile.readLine()           [1]
print(lineOne)                        [1]
myFile.close()                        [1]
```

Programming Techniques 2

1. a) 5 **[1]**
   b) 6 **[1]**
   c) Because more than one colour could begin with the same letter **[1]**
   d) bikeID **[1]**
2. a) CREATE TABLE Stock (bikeID INTEGER PRIMARY KEY, bikeBrand STRING, numberofGears INTEGER, overallWeight REAL, colourCode CHARACTER, inStock BOOLEAN); **[1]**

b) SELECT bikeID FROM Stock WHERE numberofGears > 20; **[1]**

c) SELECT bikeID FROM Stock WHERE numberofGears = 18 AND inStock = Yes; **[1]**

3. **a)** Example answer:

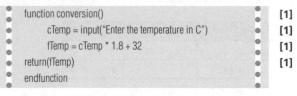

array laptime[4]	**[1]**
week[0] = "59.4"	**[1]**
week[1] = "64.3"	
week[2] = "74.3"	
week[3] = "81.9"	

   b) By adding the times of several runners **[1]**

4. To save time **[1]**, to avoid repetitive code **[1]** and to organize/structure programs **[1]**

5. Parameters refer to variables within a sub-program **[1]**, and arguments are the actual data passed to the parameters **[1]**

6. **a)** Example answer:

```
function conversion()                                    [1]
    cTemp = input("Enter the temperature in C")          [1]
    fTemp = cTemp * 1.8 + 32                             [1]
    return(fTemp)                                        [1]
endfunction
```

   b) A function will return a value; a procedure will not **[1]**

Producing Robust Programs

1. **a)** Making sure to consider all those who will be using your program **[1]** and what access each user will be given **[1]**
   b) Examples: use of usernames and passwords **[1]**; making sure children have access to relevant areas only **[1]**; considering what might happen when incorrect keys are pressed **[1]**

2. Use of comments within the program **[1]**; use of indentation **[1]**; use of well-named variables **[1]**; use of sub-routines **[1]**

3. Syntax errors are usually spotted by the program compiler and are specific to the language being used **[1]**, but logic errors are faults in the structure that cause the program to fail **[1]**

4. A logic error may be written correctly without any syntax errors **[1]** but references between lines of code may be confused and often only be spotted can by working through the program one line at a time **[1]**

5.

Iterative testing	A cycle of design, development and testing, with the results of testing fed back into the loop.
Final testing	Carried out by real users to find issues not considered by the original designer.
Performance testing	The impact the program will have on system resources when it is run.
Usability testing	An examination of how user-friendly the system is.
Security testing	How vulnerable is the program to attacks, and is the data secure?
Load/stress testing	Will the program crash if several users access it at once?

[6]

6. Extreme data tests the ranges of expected values that may be entered **[1]** and erroneous data considers incorrect entries that should not be processed **[1]**

Translators and Facilities of Languages

1. Examples: Python **[1]**; C Family **[1]**; Java **[1]**; JavaScript **[1]**; Visual Basic **[1]**; PHP **[1]**; Delphi **[1]**; SQL **[1]**; Bash **[1]**

2. Compilers **[1]** convert whole programs to machine code **[1]**. Interpreters **[1]** convert one line of code at a time to machine code **[1]**

3. Any two of the following: they may prefer the fine control and lower memory usage **[1]**; they may specifically want to focus on CPU processing **[1]**; they may be working with older devices **[1]**

4. Code is colour coded, visually highlighting errors **[1]** and language-specific coding mistakes are highlighted when the program is run **[1]**

5.

Code editors	These are designed for writing source code, with tools to assist with formatting and syntax.
Error diagnostics	Also known as debugging tools, these will help to identify errors in particular lines of code.
Run-time environment	This allows programs to be run virtually within the IDE software.
Translators	This will compile or interpret the final code as required.

[4]

6. Any three of the following: the program can be run virtually before being translated **[1]**; the position of errors will be highlighted if a program stops **[1]**; data type errors can be spotted **[1]**; sections of program can be run and checked **[1]**

Pages 183–187 Data Representation

Units and Formats of Data

1.

high-definition video	gigabytes
MP3 audio file	megabytes
system backup files	terabytes
word processing document	kilobytes

[4]

2. So that there are enough characters for all European languages **[1]** that require accents and additional symbols **[1]**

3. Unicode **[1]**

4. **a)** 163 **[1]**
   b) 247 **[1]**
   c) 75 **[1]**
   d) 33 **[1]**

5. To allow it to be used with common 8-bit systems **[1]**

6. Examples: space **[1]**; delete **[1]**; enter **[1]**; escape **[1]**; tab **[1]**

Converting Data 1

1. **a)** 00010010 **[1]**
   b) 00011001 **[1]**
   c) 11111011 **[1]**
   d) 10100001 **[1]**

2. **a)** 011101010 **[1]** or 234 **[1]**
   b) 01011001 **[1]** or 89 **[1]**

3. Example: 11111100 + 10000000 (380) [1]
4. a) 01101010 [1]
   b) 01001100 [1]
5. a) 01101010 [1]
   b) 00101101 [1]
6. To carry out multiplication and division [1]

Converting Data 2

1. a) FE [1]
   b) 63 [1]
   c) 2A [1]
2. 42 49 47 [3]
3. a) 79 [1]
   b) 140 [1]
   c) 18 [1]
4. Because long binary sequences can be shortened to a more manageable hexadecimal sequence [1]
5. They might see it as the denary number 24 rather than the characters 2 and 4 [1]
6. Check digit [1]; it uses an algorithm to check that the data is in the correct format by checking the final digital [1]

Audio/Visual Formats and Compression

1. a) 1 bit [1]
   b) 2 bits [1]
   c) 4 bits [1]
2. To catalogue data by (any two of) location [1]; date [1]; time [1]; camera settings [1]
3. Benefit: high-quality accurate recording [1]; drawback: large digital file size [1]
4. RAW is a lossless file format, so all the original image data is maintained [1]
5. The file type JPEG uses lossy compression [1], so each time the file is saved, more data is lost [1]
6. MP3 [1], because the small file size is easy to download [1]/the quality does not have to be very high [1]

Pages 188–197 Paper 1: Computer Systems

1. a) The remote storing and accessibility of files and applications via the Internet [1]
   b) i) Two advantages from the following: files can be accessed from any Internet-connected location [1]; additional devices do not need to be carried [1]; access to files can be shared with other users [1]
      ii) Two disadvantages from the following: loss of access if Internet connection is lost [1]; speed of access is determined by Internet connection [1]; access is not available in all geographical areas [1]
   c) i) Secondary storage refers to the devices used to store programs, documents and files [1]
      ii) Solid-state drive [1], because it is more durable than other devices [1]
2. a) Two reasons from the following: to update security settings [1]; to add functionality [1]; to update drivers [1]
   b) i) Random access memory is a temporary area that a computer uses to store data in current use [1]
      ii) Additional RAM means more short-term memory to carry out tasks [1], allowing the processor to run and perform better [1]
   c) i) Additional short-term memory space created by the CPU on the hard drive if RAM becomes full [1]
      ii) Advantage: creates additional RAM without replacing or adding hardware [1]. Disadvantage: removes storage space from the hard disk [1] OR access to virtual memory is not as fast as RAM [1]
      iii) Two from the following: files are moved OR grouped together [1]; empty spaces are grouped together [1]; access speed is increased [1]
3. a) i) Local area network. Computers are connected with the ability to share information in a local area [1]
      ii) A WAN could be created [1]. A router is needed to connect them [1]

b) i) Wired Equivalent Privacy (WEP) [1]; Wi-Fi Protected Access [1]; Wi-Fi Protected Access 2 [1]
   ii) WP2 [1], as it is the most recent and most secure [1]
c) i) A software-managed network within an existing physical network [1]
   ii) To ensure that those using the network cannot access the shop's network and private information [1]
4. a) i) Copyright, Designs and Patents Act 1988 [1]
      ii) The Data Protection Act 1998 [1]
      iii) Creative Commons Licensing [1]
   b) i) Lossy compression permanently removes data from files [1], whereas lossless uses an algorithm to compress data but then reconstructs it without data loss [1]
      ii) Lossless [1] should be used to preserve all original elements after editing [1]
   c) Analogue audio is converted to a digital format using sampling [1] and the higher the sampling rate [1] and bit rate [1], the higher the quality
5. a) i) The search for vulnerabilities within a system that could be exploited for criminal purposes [1]
      ii) The monitoring and recording of network traffic to make sure that any attacks can be analysed [1]
   b) i) Three reasons from the following: landfill is growing around the world [1]; the computers could be used by another user [1]; chemicals and hard-to-recycle elements can damage the environment [1]; creating new products increases greenhouse gases [1]; the transportation of products and waste causes pollution [1]
      ii) One alternative from the following: charities will repurpose machines so that they can be given to those without access [1]; the equipment can be passed on to educational establishments [1]
6. a) To flood a website or network with data traffic so that it is brought to a halt [1]
   b) i) Three pieces of advice from the following: make sure that passwords are at least eight characters long [1]; use upper- and lower-case characters [1]; include special characters (for example ?, # and %) [1]; avoid using real dictionary words [1]; avoid using any personal information [1]; regularly change any password [1]; never use the same password for more than one system [1]
      ii) By trying commonly used passwords [1] or by accessing social network information and trying passwords derived from personal information [1]
   c) i) HTTP Secure encrypts communication between server and client [1]
      ii) A set of rules to allow multiple network devices around the world to communicate [1]
   d) Three from the following: virus [1] – a program hidden within another program or file, designed to cause damage to file systems [1]; worm [1] – a malicious program that acts independently and can replicate itself and spread throughout a system [1]; Trojan [1] – installed by a user who thinks that it is a legitimate piece of software when, in fact, it will cause damage or provide access to criminals [1]; spyware [1] – secretly passes information on to a criminal without your knowledge and is often packaged with free software [1]; adware [1] – displays targeted advertising and redirects search requests without permission [1]; ransomware [1] – limits or denies a user access to their system until a ransom is paid to unlock it [1]; pharming [1] – the redirecting of a user's website – by modifying their DNS entries – to a fraudulent site without their permission [1]
7. a) Server 3 [1], as it has the highest number of cores [1] and the largest hard drive space [1]
   b) Two advantages from the following: the failure of one device, as long as it is not the server, will not affect the rest of the network [1]; the network can be expanded by adding devices until the server capacity is reached [1]; localized problems can be identified quickly [1]; data can be directed to a specific address via the central server, reducing traffic [1]

Two disadvantages from the following: if the server fails, then the whole network will collapse [1]; extensive cabling is required [1]; a high level of technical knowledge is required to maintain the server [1]

c) New software can be easily installed on the central server for all students [1]; low-specification client machines can be added or replaced at low cost as the number of students expands [1]; security and network access can be controlled from the network's central location [1]

8. a) The conversion of important data into a form that cannot be read without a key [1]

b) Data is broken down into small pieces called packets [1]; the most efficient route is taken by each individual packet [1]; the data is transmitted and then reassembled at its destination [1]

9. **Mark Band 3 – High Level (6–8 marks)**
Level of detail:
Thorough knowledge and understanding. Wide range of considerations in relation to question. Response is accurate and detailed. Application of knowledge with evidence/examples related to question. Both sides of discussion carefully considered.

Mark Band 2 – Mid Level (3–5 marks)
Level of detail:
Reasonable knowledge and understanding. Range of considerations in relation to question. Response is generally accurate. Application of knowledge relates to content. Discussion of most areas.

Mark Band 1 – Low Level (1–2 marks)
Level of detail:
Basic knowledge and understanding. Limited consideration in relation to question with basic responses. Limited application of knowledge and basic discussion of content.

Content will include:
- Security
  - Making sure that users cannot access secure information outside that required by their role
  - Use of strong/regularly changing/non-repeated passwords
  - Users are accessing secure financial information
- Employee responsibilities
  - Access records checked and monitored
  - Not sharing login/password details
  - Not sharing any information read in or outside the workplace
- Fraud
  - Preventing personal information being accessed by external users
  - Danger of phishing scams, even within an organisation
  - Access to financial transactions
- Legislation
  - Data Protection Act – ensuring that details are secure and up to date
  - Computer Misuse Act – accessing secure information and sharing or using it to commit crime. External danger of malware

Pages 198–209 Paper 2: Computational Thinking, Algorithms and Programming

1. a) TB [1]
b) 11111001 [1]
c) 259 doesn't fit into 8 bits, so the computer tries to process more bits than it is designed to handle [1]
d) 010011110 [1], 158 [1]

e) 233 [2]
f) i) Example:

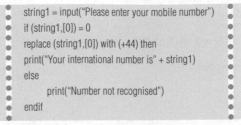

```
string1 = input("Please enter your mobile number")
if (string1,[0]) = 0
replace (string1,[0]) with (+44) then
print("Your international number is" + string1)
else
        print("Number not recognised")
endif
```

(1 mark – input; 1 mark – string; 1 mark – if; 1 mark – replace number; 1 mark – else) [Total 5]
ii) String [1]

2. a) A record is a single row or entry of related data in a database [1]; a field is a database category within a record [1]

b) i)

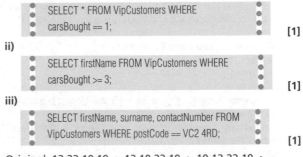

```
SELECT * FROM VipCustomers WHERE
carsBought == 1;
```
[1]

ii)

```
SELECT firstName FROM VipCustomers WHERE
carsBought >= 3;
```
[1]

iii)

```
SELECT firstName, surname, contactNumber FROM
VipCustomers WHERE postCode == VC2 4RD;
```
[1]

3. a) Original: 13,32,10,19 -> 13,10,32,19 -> 10,13,32,19 -> 10,13,19,32 [3]
b) Check the first item 10 = 13 False, check the second item 10 = 32 False, check the third item 10 = 10 Correct [3]
c) Binary search [1]

4. Example:
a) i)

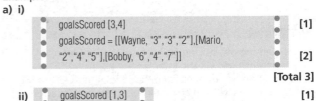

```
goalsScored [3,4]                                    [1]
goalsScored = [[Wayne, "3","3","2"],[Mario,
"2","4","5"],[Bobby, "6","4","7"]]                   [2]
```
[Total 3]

ii) `goalsScored [1,3]` [1]

b) A one-dimensional array can only hold a single list of common elements [1]

5. a) diceOne [1], diceTwo [1]
b) Is diceOne exactly equal to diceTwo? [2]
c) i) A section of code that can be called at any time during that program to save time and avoid repetition [1]
ii) Example:

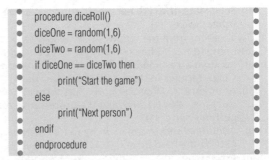

```
procedure diceRoll()
diceOne = random(1,6)
diceTwo = random(1,6)
if diceOne == diceTwo then
        print("Start the game")
else
        print("Next person")
endif
endprocedure
```

(1 mark – procedure; 1 mark – if; 1 mark – correct terminology) [Total 3]
iii) Procedure [1]

c) i) A programming language, such as Python or Java, that uses keywords and syntax that programmers can understand [1]

ii) Assemblers [1] are required to convert low-level languages, such as assembly language, into instructions [1]; compilers [1] are used to read high-level languages and convert programs as a whole into machine code programs [1]; interpreters [1] are used to examine a high-level language file one line at a time and convert each instruction into compatible machine code instructions [1] [Total 6]

6. a) i)

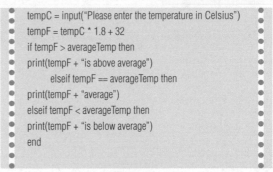

(1 mark for each shape in correct location) [Total 3]

ii)

A	B	C	X
0	0	0	0
0	0	1	0
0	1	0	1
0	1	1	0
1	0	0	1
1	0	1	0
1	1	0	1
1	1	1	0

(1 mark for each row) [Total 8]

b) Both inputs A AND B [1] must be turned off [1] to produce a positive output at Z

7. a) Decomposition [1] and abstraction [1]

b) By using comments to add notes in her coding [1]

c) Example:

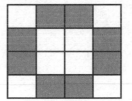

```
tempC = input("Please enter the temperature in Celsius")
tempF = tempC * 1.8 + 32
if tempF > averageTemp then
    print(tempF + "is above average")
        elseif tempF == averageTemp then
    print(tempF + "average")
    elseif tempF < averageTemp then
    print(tempF + "is below average")
    end
```

(1 mark – comparison operators; 1 mark – if; 1 mark – else; 1 mark – using original program) [Total 4]

d) Normal data [1], which is acceptable data likely to be input into the program [1]; extreme (or boundary) data [1], which is values at the limit of what a program should be able to handle [1]; erroneous (or invalid) data [1], which is values that the program should not accept or process [1]

8. a) Binary sequence: 01101001 10010110 [1]

(1 mark for each line) [Total 4]

b) 16 [1]

c) One each from the following:
Advantage: files can be downloaded quickly [1]; small file sizes mean less storage capacity is used [1]
Disadvantage: quality/fine detail can be lost [1]; original image cannot be restored [1]

Notes

Notes

Notes

GCSE Computer Science

Notes

Collins GCSE Revision

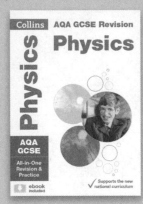

Physics — AQA GCSE Revision

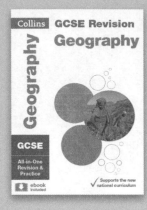

Geography — GCSE Revision

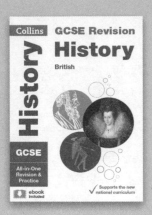

History — GCSE Revision, British

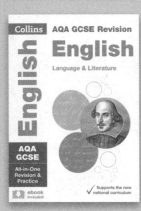

English — AQA GCSE Revision, Language & Literature

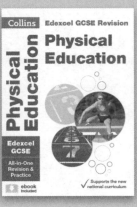

Physical Education — Edexcel GCSE Revision

Maths — Edexcel GCSE Revision, Foundation

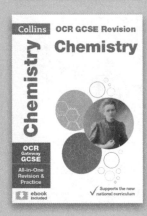

Chemistry — OCR GCSE Revision

French — AQA GCSE Revision, with Audio

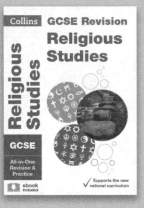

Religious Studies — GCSE Revision

Spanish — AQA GCSE Revision, with Audio

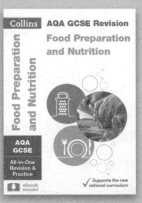

Food Preparation and Nutrition — AQA GCSE Revision

Biology — OCR GCSE Revision

Visit the website to view the complete range and place an order:

www.collins.co.uk/collinsGCSErevision

ACKNOWLEDGEMENTS

The author and publisher are grateful to the copyright holders for permission to use quoted materials and images.

Cover, P.1, P.145 © Alexey Kotelnikov/Alamy
All other images © Shutterstock.com

Every effort has been made to trace copyright holders and obtain their permission for the use of copyright material. The author and publisher will gladly receive information enabling them to rectify any error or omission in subsequent editions. All facts are correct at time of going to press.

Published by Collins

An imprint of HarperCollins*Publishers* Ltd

1 London Bridge Street,
London, SE1 9GF

© HarperCollins*Publishers* Limited

9780008227470

First published 2017

10 9 8 7 6 5 4 3 2 1

All rights reserved. No part of this publication may be reproduced, stored in a retrieval system, or transmitted, in any form or by any means, electronic, mechanical, photocopying, recording or otherwise, without the prior permission of Collins.

British Library Cataloguing in Publication Data.

A CIP record of this book is available from the British Library.

Authored by: Paul Clowrey
Commissioning Editors: Katherine Wilkinson and Charlotte Christensen
Editor: Charlotte Christensen
Project Manager: Katrina Strachan, Prepress Projects
Cover Design: Sarah Duxbury and Paul Oates
Inside Concept Design: Sarah Duxbury and Paul Oates
Text Design and Layout: Jouve India Private Limited
Production: Natalia Rebow
Printed in the UK by Bell and Bain Ltd, Glasgow

HarperCollins PUBLISHERS — *Since 1817* — 200

6 EASY WAYS TO ORDER

1. Available from www.collins.co.uk
2. Fax your order to 01484 665736
3. Phone us on 0844 576 8126
4. Email us at education@harpercollins.co.uk
5. Post your order to: Collins Education, FREEPOST RTKB-SGZT-ZYJL, Honley HD9 6QZ
6. Or visit your local bookshop.